Bushwhacked

Coping with the American Superpower
And Other Post-Cold War Dilemmas

Michael B. Davie

Manor House Publishing Inc.

Manor House Publishing Inc.
(905) 648-2193

National Library of Canada
Cataloguing in Publication Data:

Davie, Michael B., 1954-
Bushwhacked
Coping with the American Superpower
and other Post-Cold War Dilemmas / Michael B. Davie.

Includes bibliographical references and notes.
ISBN 0-9731956-1-4

1. World politics – 1989- 2. International trade. 3. Canada – Foreign relations – 1945- 4. Canada – Foreign economic relations. 5. United States – Foreign relations – 1989- 6. United States – Foreign relations – 1989- 6. United States – Foreign economic relations. I. Title.

E895.D39 2002   327'.09'049   C'2002-905157-6

Published November 15, 2002
by Manor House Publishing: (905) 648-2193

Printed in Canada by Webcom Limited.
First Edition. 2 parts. 4 chapters. 128 pages.

Cover concept/design: Michael B. Davie.
Cover layout/realization: Richard Kosydar.
Cover photograph: Courtesy AP/Wide World Photos.
Please note: The Associated Press does not necessarily endorse the book's content or share the author's views.

By Michael B. Davie:

All titles published by Manor House Publishing Inc., unless indicated otherwise.

Non-fiction

Bush**whacked**
Coping with the American Superpower
and other Post-Cold War Dilemmas

Winning Ways
Vol. 1: The Right Stuff

Following The Great Spirit
Exploring Native Indian Belief Systems

Political Losers
In Canada, U.S., Ukraine

Distant Voices
Canadian Politics On the Outside Looking In

Canada Decentralized
Can Our Nation Survive?

Quebec and Section 33
Why The Notwithstanding Clause Must Not Stand

Inside the Witches' Coven
Exploring Wiccan Rituals

Enterprise 2000
Hamilton, Halton, Niagara Embrace the Millennium

Success Stories BR
Business Achievement in Greater Hamilton

Hamilton: It's Happening * BR
Celebrating Hamilton's Sesquicentennial

Fiction

You're on my hit list for calling me
Creep
A Novel

The Late Man
A Novel

Archival

Print History
(Self-published, with more than 60 volumes and over 10,000 pieces of published writings)

BR = Published by BRaSH Publishing
* = With co-author Sherry Sleightholm

Acknowledgements

This book would not have been possible without the thoughtful, analytical works of political scientists more seasoned and insightful than I.
I am grateful for the expert teachings of the political scientists I've cited in this book and for the patient distilling of knowledge by my McMaster University professors who helped me to earn honours degrees in Political Science.
As well, I appreciate the assistance extended by many conscientious people, too numerous to mention, in bringing this book to fruition.
My thanks, as always, to my wife Philippa for her constant encouragement and faith in the validity of my misadventures.

- Michael B. Davie.

For
Philippa

About the author

One of Canada's most intriguing and prolific writers, Michael B. Davie is the author of critically acclaimed business books Winning Ways, Enterprise 2000 and Success Stories.

The award-winning writer is also the author of nationally important books Distant Voices, Political Losers, Canada Decentralized and Quebec & Section 33: Why the Notwithstanding Clause Must Not Stand. He also wrote The Late Man, his 10th book and first novel.

Davie has even explored the supernatural in his books Inside The Witches' Coven and Following The Great Spirit.

Michael B. Davie is also a journalist with The Toronto Star, Canada's largest newspaper, reaching millions of readers daily.

The author has won dozens of awards for outstanding journalism. His work has also appeared in such major Canadian newspapers as the Halifax Chronicle-Herald, Montreal Gazette, Calgary Herald, Winnipeg Free Press, Edmonton Journal and The Vancouver Sun.

Prior to The Star, he was an editor with The Globe and Mail, Canada's national newspaper with coast-to-coast readership.

Previous to The Globe, he spent 17 years with The Hamilton Spectator, where he won 28 journalism awards.

Prior to joining The Spectator, he spent five years with other publications, including the daily Welland Tribune where he was a reporter, columnist and editor.

He also served two years as regional news editor for one of Ontario's largest chains of community newspapers.

Born in Hamilton in 1954, Michael B. Davie's interest in writing began in early childhood. As a pre-school child, he became withdrawn and was in a state of shock after his parents decided to divorce. During a visit to a community centre, the child opened the door to a room to find child psychologists had been busy studying him through two-way mirrors.

The young child then began closely observing other children and adults, studying their interaction and watching their stories unfold. By the late 1960s and into the 1970s, while in his teens, he was a regular contributing writer to counter culture publications.

He turned professional in the mid-1970s as Editor of The Phoenix serving Mohawk College of Applied Arts & Technology where he went on to earn a Broadcast Journalism diploma.

The author also holds a Niagara College Print Journalism diploma and degrees in Political Science from McMaster University where he was repeatedly named to the Deans' Honour List and won the Political Science Prize for outstanding academic achievement.

Michael B. Davie currently resides in Ancaster with his wife Philippa and their children Donovan, Sarah and Ryan.

Manor House Publishing Inc.
(905) 648-2193.

Contents

"The Americans are our best friends – whether we like it or not."
- Canadian Prime Minister Jean Chretien

Part One

Bushwhacked

"Those who are not with us are with the terrorists."
- U.S. President George W. Bush

"When it comes to free trade, U.S. President George Bush is two-faced, unwilling to exert the type of focused consistent political leadership he has demonstrated in the war against terrorism... If a foreign nation pursued the Janus-faced trade policies coming out of his administration, George W. Bush would yell foul."
- **Avrum D. Lank,**
The Milwaukee Journal Sentinel

Chapter One

Trouble on the Trade Front

U.S. Superpower relations post September 11

Sept. 11, 2001: Images forever burned into our collective consciousness: The sight of jets smashing into the World Trade Center in New York. The sight of these twin towers collapsing into piles of burning, twisted metal.

Canada responded quickly, tightening our own security while rerouting aircraft in U.S. skies into our own airspace.

This move was at considerable risk: At that time, it was not known if there were terrorists aboard other aircraft. Canada and Canadians put their own safety and security at risk by welcoming these remaining jets into our airspace and airports.

We responded with heartfelt sympathy for the victims – mainly Americans but with some Canadians and other nationals – with national memorials and ceremonies.

Virtually all Canadians viewed the events of 9-11 with shock and revulsion. While many of us disagree with much of U.S. foreign policies and U.S. dealings with other countries, as a nation we were revolted by the shockingly horrific 9-11 acts of terrorism on our friends.

Whatever the U.S. may have done abroad in terms of insensitivity or bullying other nations, nothing justified this assault on a purely civilian target: twin commercial towers filled solely with working civilians and tourists (the attack on the Pentagon, while regrettable, was at least more justifiable from a military standpoint given that it is the nerve centre for the American military).

That said, it is astonishing that the U.S. would continue its isolating, and isolationist, unilateral approach with its allies in the free world.

If 9-11 taught the Americans nothing else, it ought to have conveyed the message that the U.S. is not invincible. It is not invulnerable. It needs the support of other countries. It cannot go it alone and always expect absolute success.

Right up until 9-11, George W. Bush, the American president who came in second – but still got to move into the White House, had been desperately trying to shore up domestic support.

This was difficult to do with the majority of Americans preferring his opponent Al Gore (the Democrat obtained around half a million more votes. But Bush won in a contest fraught with voting irregularities).

Shoring up domestic support was also difficult to do with the U.S. economy faltering.

Bush also found himself without the votes necessary to ram through his hastily concocted policies and ill-conceived tax cuts in the midst of rising unemployment and a health care crisis (and when one Republican senator left the party, Bush would increasingly find himself without sufficient support to carry out his agenda, until regaining Senate control in the November 2002 elections) .

But the American political system does in fact allow its presidents considerable room to manoeuvre when it comes to international politics – even when it comes to declaring war.

For the most part still a novice at world politics, Bush still wasted no time in shedding the domestic strait jacket to take advantage of the opportunity to throw his weight around abroad.

Within days of taking office, Bush flexed America's military muscle and forcibly enforced the no-fly zone in Iraq

Then he started throwing his weight around elsewhere internationally. Indeed, several important treaties were either cancelled, ignored or disregarded as flawed by the U.S. as it sought to prove that it was so powerful it could say and do anything without repercussions. The message – in large type – was that the U.S. would represent U.S. interests to exclusion of everything else, so shut-up and listen.

It's difficult to say what kind of mileage Republican spin doctors were able to extract from the president's adventures abroad, but it would appear that international politics presented the one forum where Bush could appear simultaneously effective and in charge.

Indeed, Bush strode the world stage like a bull in a china shop, knocking over delicate agreements, years in the making, while he barrelled straight ahead, purely representing U.S. interests. Full speed ahead. Diplomacy be damned.

Canada found itself slapped with trade penalties over the softwood lumber sales made to American customers.

We were placed at risk of getting penalized for our steel trade.

We hadn't done anything wrong – but we were bushwhacked nonetheless.

Then 9-11 happened. A shaken America was forced to re-examine its self-appointed role as the world's New Rome. Its new enemy was potentially anywhere – and everywhere.

Americans looked to their president for an effective response, and in fairness, Bush rose admirably to the challenge.

But over time, his inexperience and lack of statesmanship have again become an issue.

Bush has stubbornly insisted that highly complex matters involving cultural/religious differences and perceived potential threats from abroad are simply – simplistically – black or white.

However, thinking people everywhere have had difficulty buying into his assertions that he should be given a blank cheque to do whatever he feels like, to attack any country he deems a threat, to artlessly divide the world into good guys and bad guys (with some of the 'good guys' being brutal dictatorships that happen to support the U.S. – at the moment).

The New Rome is playing its fiddle loudly. But fewer people are listening. They're trying to tune out the racket and think for themselves, develop their own foreign policies, policies that take much more into account than purely U.S. interests.

Life wasn't always this complicated.

As Toronto Star political columnist Richard Gwyn notes, during the Cold War, most of the world was polarized, with a good many nations 'belonging' to the U.S. or the Soviet Union. In short, they were allied with "one of two heavily armed camps that were separated from each other by fear, suspicion and hatred." [1.]

Gwyn goes on to observe that less than 15 years after the end of the Cold War, the world is again polarized, and this time the division is between "those countries that the U.S. says are harbouring or supporting terrorists and those countries the U.S. says are fighting terrorism." 2.

In other words, whether or not a nation is actually harbouring terrorists or is instead fighting terrorists is less important than whether the U.S., which now sets all the rules in the New World Order, recognizes and accepts their particular role.

Gwyn asserts that this judge and jury role assumed by the U.S. was apparent in the State of the Union address U.S. President George W. Bush delivered in late January 2002.

As Gwyn observes:

> "In his first TV address after Sept. 11, Bush laid down the rule that "those who are not with us are with the terrorists." This time (the State of the Union address), he took his own rule and applied it wherever and to whomever he chose." 3.

But in this same speech, Bush stated Iraq, Iran and North Korea constitute an "axis of evil," an interesting assertion since Iraq and Iran are historically enemies and there is little evidence of either nation communicating with Korea (in this regard, we Canadians are not blameless as the 'axis of evil' remark was actually concocted by Bush's Canadian speech writer David Frum, a journalist and son of the late great CBC broadcaster Barbara Frum).

Worse, the assertion comes after a moderate and increasingly democratic Iran provided the U.S. with intelligence and moral support in the War on Terrorism.

North Korea has been preoccupied with peaceful overtures from South Korea and the conflict in that part of the world shows signs of being resolved peacefully.

Although Iraq still hates the States, it is weakened from sanctions and poses little threat to the U.S. Gwyn, however, suspects that the list is somewhat political in nature, with non-Muslim North Korea included so nobody can accuse the U.S. of waging a 'crusade' against the Muslim countries and with Iran included to express U.S. disapproval of an Iranian arms shipment to the Palestinians. 4.

As terrible as Sept. 11 was, it appears to have given the U.S. the justification needed to continue as a military superpower.

Gwyn observes:

> "In one way of another, the U.S. has been on a war footing for more than a half-century now, from the immediate post-World War II period and the start of the Cold War, with only a brief semi-retirement after the Cold War ended. Through terrorism, Bush has found a way to perpetuate America's militarization. This one is going to go on and on for decades, perhaps another half-century." 5.

Not that I fault the prolonged U.S.-led fight against terrorism – far from it. Although U.S. policy in the Middle East may be criticized by some as insensitive and deemed unfair in some Muslim quarters, nothing the U.S. has ever done could possible justify the horrific and cowardly Sept. 11 attacks.

It is also truly despicable that innocent civilians were deliberately targeted by fanatical organizations that lacked the basic guts to take responsibility for their acts. It was only months later that a videotaped bragging session showed Osama bin Laden indicating he knew well of the attacks and indeed orchestrated them.

Perhaps more disturbing than bin Laden's musings are the findings of a recent Gallop Poll – released in March 2002 – of countries throughout the Islamic world. The poll revealed massive hatred of the United States among many Muslims.

More than half of the nearly 10,000 Muslims surveyed detested George W. Bush and found the U.S. to be arrogant and ruthless.

More than three-quarters deem the Allies' attacks on Al Qaeda and the Taliban to be unjustified. The underlying message seems to be: Just leave the terrorists alone – and get out of the Middle East while you're at it. Most incredibly, nearly two-thirds said they don't believe Arab terrorist groups were behind the Sept. 11, 2001, attacks.

Noting most of those who did not believe Arab terrorists were at fault also tended to blame the Israeli Mossad secret service, Richard Gwyn concludes: "This is denial of reality (as well as a self-absolution of the consequences of condoning, or at the very least of the accepting of religious fanaticism), on a massive, and a psychologically unbalanced scale." 6.

Gwyn also notes that the Muslim world can be described as a failed continent, which has fallen behind the rest of the world, a continent in which the resident intellectuals must go elsewhere to allow their "intellects to soar." 7.

Indeed, the Muslim world, in general, is an entity where corrupt, incompetent, ruthless and oppressive, self-serving, undemocratic regimes reign supreme over illiterate, ignorant populations awash in grinding poverty.

And it's these same illiterate, redneck populations that are prone to rise up as massive mobs to blame their failings on the West and vent their venom on non-believers (of their brand of religion).

Since much of this seems to be driven by an irrational hatred of the successful West, it appears unlikely any trustworthy, negotiated resolutions are possible with such regimes and populations.

The U.S.-led allies would therefore appear to have little choice but to attempt to eradicate terrorism wherever they find it.

In this fight, Canada was the first nation to offer the U.S. tangible help on Sept. 11, 2001. Our nation opened our airspace and airports to diverted U.S. flights – taking on the enormous risk that we could be bringing terrorist-controlled aircraft into our own country.

We were also among the first to fully support the War on Terrorism. We also tightened up our borders and Canadian soldiers were soon fighting shoulder-to-shoulder alongside Americans.

Given this, you might think a grateful U.S. would be looking at ways of thanking Canada for our immediate, unconditional support.

In fact, the evidence is entirely to the contrary. The U.S. shows an increased penchant for ignoring free trade agreements and slapping trade penalties on any trade where Canadians appear to have the upper hand – steel and softwood lumber in particular – despite any real evidence that we're somehow trading unfairly.

A Toronto Star editorial neatly captured the very essence of blatant U.S. isolationism and unilateralism on the trade front when it noted that despite the existence of two free trade agreements, Canada has been forced again and again to take the U.S. before the World Trade Organization to protest sky-high tariffs on Canadian exports of softwood lumber.

As The Star observes: "Washington is now following its attack on our softwood with threats to our wheat farmers and steelmakers… Canada could also get hit by the scattergun Washington is waving at foreign steel producers everywhere, who it blames for a glut of steel over-hanging its market… This is not free trade. What we have is as much trade as the U.S. is prepared to allow." 8.

A slapping of tariffs on Canada's beleaguered; fair-trading steel industry would have devastating impact on the nation's steel capital of Hamilton.

Such duties would make the Canadian-made steel more expensive than steel produced in the U.S. costing Hamilton's steelmakers customers and sales in the process.

Fortunately, Canada dodged that bullet when the Ontario and federal governments joined the news media in complaining about America's tendency to ignore the free trade agreements it freely negotiated with our nation.

The pressure appears to have paid off: Citing the free trade agreements, the U.S., in March 2002, slapped duties as high as 30 per cent on an array of steel-producing countries – but spared Canada. 9.

However some of the countries hit by duties charge the move is nothing more than a protectionist U.S. effort to prop up its own failing steel industries by claiming any steel sold more cheaply to the U.S. must be dumped (sold below the production cost of the steel in the originating country).

In some cases – Russia, China, South Korea – the steel likely is being dumped. But other countries are clearly concerned over what they deem a unilateral, anti-trade move. As Hamilton Spectator business writer Steve Arnold notes:

> "World reaction to the American decision was highly critical, with Britain and the European Union warning of retaliation for an action which raises the issue of import diversion, threatening jobs across Europe. A European challenge of the action before the World Trade Organization is one potential response." 10.

Indeed, many nations in the world – Canada is often among them – are worried by an American tendency to protect its own interests regardless of the fact that innocent nations may be hurt in the process.

In trade disputes, it seems, the other guy is too often to be deemed guilty by the U.S. unless he can prove himself innocent.

However, criticism of self-serving, one-sided American trade policies is also being increasingly voiced in the U.S. itself.

For example, in May of 2002, the U.S. reversed itself from a 1996 law that was intended to reduce farmer's dependence on federal aid and decided to spend $190 billion US on farm subsidies, primarily to large farms that don't need such support.

The outrageous move quickly prompted widespread objections without and within the U.S., including this missive from Forth Worth Star-Telegram columnist Bob Ray Sanders:

> "You can call it aid or subsidy or price guarantees. But let's call the new farm bill exactly what it is. Welfare. Big-time welfare. Mostly for those who need it the least. The United States is good about giving assistance to large corporations while cutting benefits to individuals who are really in need." 11.

Sanders is also alarmed that the U.S. is deliberately and unnecessarily antagonizing its trading partners:

> "European trading partners, already upset with the United States for newly imposed tariffs on steel, are very troubled over this latest move to prop up American Farmers and ranchers. Canadian Agriculture Minister Lyle Vanclief has also been critical of the American subsidies. There's talk in capitals around the world of launching a formal World Trade Organization complaint against the United States over the subsidy package. At the rate the U.S. is going, it might be inciting new trade wars and that is definitely something it does not need." 12.

Toronto Star economics columnist David Crane is also concerned of a potential trade war.

Crane notes: "U.S. measures – on softwood lumber, steel and huge new subsidies for American farmers – also threaten the pace of global economic recovery because other countries are tempted to retaliate, triggering a global trade war that would slow economic growth and trigger higher unemployment." 13.

As Crane also observes:

> "Canadians have felt the costly impact of U.S. protectionism through the penalties applied against softwood lumber producers, throwing many thousands of Canadians out of work. But Canadian anger, though strong, seems mild compared to European reaction to the trade penalties its steel producers now face – penalties averaging 30 per cent. What is especially galling is that the George W. Bush administration is taking a variety of destructive protectionist measures to win votes in states where political competition is tight, and it really doesn't care how the rest of the world reacts... But with the United States acting in such a protectionist way, it is hard to see how it can speak with credibility about the benefits of trade or globalization. Its actions don't match its words." 14.

This America-first attitude, to the extent it exists on the trade front, is even more disconcerting in the military context.

Alarmed over growing U.S. isolationism and unilateralism, American historian Jeremy Brecher has gone so far as to plead with the rest of the world to rein the U.S. in.

Brecher notes the U.S. decision to withdraw from the Anti-Ballistic Missile (ABM) Treaty now threatens to ignite a new arms race, with China increasing its nuclear arsenal in response to a perceived threat from the U.S., a move which could in turn prompt India to build up its nuclear defences, which could in turn prompt the same move from Pakistan and so on and so on. 15.

Nor is it safe to assume the U.S. is even effectively running the show. As Brecher notes:

> "It is an illusion to believe the U.S. is in any way in control of events. Consider the Mideast peace process. Just as Bush and (U.S. Secretary of State Colin) Powell were rolling out a major peace initiative, the war parties in Israel and Palestine sabotaged it completely. The U.S. then tilted wildly toward the very forces in Israel that sabotaged the U.S. initiative." 16

Brecher warns: "The issue is now an emerging world crisis provoked by a superpower that is acting without rational consideration of the effects of its actions. The number of additional civil and international wars it may stir up is simply incalculable – and certainly is not being rationally calculated by the Bush administration. This represents a new stage in what it means to be the world's only superpower." 17.

Brecher says the U.S. is drunk with power and totally out of control, doing whatever it wants regardless of what other nations say:

> "Internal constraints? There is something that peoples and governments around the world need to understand: There are currently no effective internal constraints on what the existing Bush administration can or will do. Because of popular response to the Sept. 11 attacks, the administration feels – correctly, at least for a time – that it can do anything without having to fear dissent or opposition. It withdrew from the ABM treaty with barely a ripple of public questioning. Its firm endorsement of Prime Minister Ariel Sharon's controversial attacks on the Palestinian Authority wins over-whelming Congressional support. Open advocacy of a military attack and occupation of Iraq causes no stir." 18.

Although the U.S. expects its allies to walk in lockstep, Brecher says these same allies have much to lose: "The U.S. in the Cold War era at least purported to be protecting its allies. But today, as the U.S. projects its power unilaterally, its friends and allies are the ones most likely to feel the blowback from destabilization in the form of terrorism, refugees, recession and war." 19.

Brecher is calling on America's friends and allies to stand up the Bush juggernaut, question its rational and contain its rash actions before the world is plunged into global war.

He argues that the U.S. is less likely to lunge recklessly into attacking other countries if it believes there is insufficient international support for such actions. 20.

As Brecher concludes:

> "It is up to governments and civil society outside the U.S. to put constraints on what it does – both for their own sake and for America's... (Friends) Restraining the Bush administration is anything but anti-American. In fact, it is the best thing America's friends can do for us right now... Please: America's friends need to take the car keys away, until this power-drunk superpower sobers up." 21.

Political commentator and Toronto Star columnist, the late great Dalton Camp is one Canadian who fully recognized that a degree of healthy criticism of our powerful neighbour in no way amounts to disloyalty to an ally.

Camp noted most so-called Anti-American Canadians are actually fond of most Americans – but detest the self-righteous U.S. politicians who advocate heavy-handedly bombing Panama City and killing many civilians to get at a drug lord; or maintaining trade sanctions against the even less threatening Cuba, while embracing Vietnam.

Nor was Camp willing to accept that Sept. 11 has somehow made the past irrelevant and that all Canadians should now embrace all things American. As he notes:

> "The past, however, has been a learning experience in our Canadian struggle to build our own society, one that reflects our values, as we create the imperatives and priorities in our ongoing development of a distinctive Canadian democracy." 22.

In my view, Camp truly recognized the fundamental strength of Canada and correlating weakness of the United States: Canada takes pains to understand the other country's position and works to achieve lasting pacts that are mutually satisfactory 'win-win' arrangements.

In contrast, the U.S. tends to myopically look after its own interests only and doesn't even rule out using its awesome military power to force a 'win-lose' arrangement that fosters resentment, even hatred toward the U.S.

Camp was also wary of the accelerated trend toward U.S. isolationism:

> "It was only last May (2001) when the United Nations voted the United States out of a seat on the United Nations Human Rights Commission. Swept away by anger and seized by paranoia, the American government and media were quick to condemn the institution, which the U.S. politicians held in contempt and whose U.N. dues had long been allowed to remain in default. Soon after, the American leadership rejected the Kyoto Protocol on the environment, as it had refused to even join in the protocol – signed even by Afghanistan – calling for an embargo on the spread of anti-personnel mines. As of Sept. 10, the Bush administration had pretty well withdrawn from world affairs, isolating itself by deliberate choice from any thought or concern for the global terrorism that was then believed to be someone else's worry." 23.

Bush clearly needs to wake up and realize his one-sided approach to world politics simply doesn't work.

But all signs suggest things are going to get worse before they get better.

Bush seems very determined to attack Iraq, even though he had no evidence linking Iraq to the Sept. 11, 2001 terrorist attacks on America.

Perhaps more disturbing still, Bush has strengthened his blind, one-sided support for Israel to the extent that he now refuses to deal with Palestinian leader Yasser Arafat.

Bush also advocated the removal Arafat, a democratically elected leader/

Buch also is openly urged the Palestinians to vote in new leadership that is not tainted by support for terrorism.

Although there is some evidence that Arafat has given financial support to suicide bombers, he is still the Palestinian leader and his people have also suffered in this conflict.

Although certainly not without sympathy for American frustration, the rest of the world has recognized Bush's move for what it is: Gross interference with the democratic process and a complete and utter disregard for Palestine's right to sovereignty.

The United Nations, along with Canada, Great Britain, France and other nations were quick to condemn the move, noting Palestinians should be free to elect their own leader without undue interference from the United States or anyone else: The U.S should not dictate the election.

Incredibly, at the G-8 Summit of world leaders at Kananaskis in June 2002, Bush went a step further.

Bush reportedly stated that even if Arafat should win the elections (he did), he would still single-mindedly refuse to negotiate with him. 24.

Several analysts have gone so far as to deem Bush's stance as a gift to Osama bin Laden as this position would seem to support bin Laden's assertion that the U.S. and Israel are walking in lockstep with one another.

The stance appeared unlikely to achieve anything more than enrage the democratic world and further fuel Islamic militancy. 25.

All of this has led Toronto Star foreign affairs columnist Gordon Barthos to wonder if Bush has ever taken a good look at Arafat's rivals, including one Abdel Sattar Qassem, a political scientist who "does not recognize the State of Israel, admires terror bombers and supports the return of millions of refugees to Israel proper." 26.

Barthos notes other candidates are either in jail or are just simply "tainted by the very violence and corruption that Bush denounced when he demanded Arafat's head." 27.

As Barthos dryly asserts: "Given Arafat's main competition, some may even want to cheer him to the finish line." 28.

Part of the problem seems to be that Bush may understand domestic American politics but he appears to have little real comprehension of world politics and seems to assume that whatever he says, goes, no matter how many times he's proven wrong.

On this front, Bush could stand to take a lesson from Canada, which encountered and dealt with its own terrorists when Quebec separatist FLQ forces blew up mail boxes and kidnapped and killed a British diplomat.

While still going after the terrorists, the Canadian government also tackled the root causes of the unhappiness that had led to the terrorism: Efforts were made to ensure a fairer role for French Canadians in the Canadian economy.

As Toronto Star columnist Chantal Hebert says of the Canadian experience:

> "On a small scale, it goes some way to show that when it comes to rooting out terrorism, investing in social justice and allowing local democracy to take its course will achieve longer-lasting results than state repression and pre-imposed election outcomes." 29.

But then again, that's really how Canada functions.

Our national character is that of a fair-minded nation that seeks to peacefully resolve conflicts through negotiation and appeasement.

This approach is borne partly of necessity. Without massive military power at our disposal, we are denied the easy option of throwing our weight around to extract short-term gains.

Instead, we strive to truly understand our opponent's position and work with them to strike a deal both sides can live with.

The Canadian Way respects other cultures

and countries and seeks to the full extent possible to accommodate them.

This is how we turn foreigners into friends. This is how we create trade "partners" in the truest sense of the word.

Getting the better of a deal at the other party's expense may provide short-term gains but it's bound to come back and haunt you when the other party eventually figures out a way to get back at you to exact some form of revenge for a deal or slight you may have long forgotten. The United States has indulged in 'win-lose deal-making for far too long.

Canada's approach can transform potential enemies into allies who appreciate our nation's unwillingness to unduly exploit the weaknesses of others, or to use our clout to impoverish others while enriching ourselves.

In essence, we don't feel we've won a good deal until the other party feels they've also won.

This approach creates meaningful long-term agreements with sustainable benefits. And it's an approach the United States would be well advised to take.

End Notes:

1. Richard Gwyn, 'U.S. military, George Bush and the new world order', The Toronto Star, pg. A13, February 3, 2002.
2. IBID.
3. IBID.
4. IBID.
5. IBID.
6. IBID
7. Richard Gwyn, 'Moderate Muslims on the offensive', The Toronto Star, March 3, 2002, pg. A13.
8. The Toronto Star, Pg. A16, January 28, 2002.
9. Steve Arnold, The Hamilton Spectator, March 6, 2002, pg. C6.
10. IBID.
11. Bob Ray Sanders, 'Welfare for big American farmers', The Fort Worth Star-Telegram, May 7, 2002. Pg. A16.
12. IBID.
13. David Crane, 'U.S. fast losing credibility as free trader', The Toronto Star, May 16, 2002. Pg. C2.
14. IBID.
15. Jeremy Brecher, 'To U.S. friends: Stop us please. Take keys away from this drunk superpower soon', The Hamilton Spectator, January 25, 2002.
16. IBID.

17. IBID.
18. IBID.
19. IBID.
20. IBID.
21. IBID.
22. Dalton Camp, 'We like Americans but not their politics', The Toronto Star, Oct. 3, 2001, pg. A21.
23. IBID.
24. The Toronto Star, 'Bush: "I meant what I said', June 27, 2002. p. A1 and A10.
25. Reuters News Agency, 'Bush speech 'God's gift to bin Laden', The Toronto Star, June 28, 2002. p. A10.
26. Gordon Barthos, 'Loathe Arafat? Try Qassem', The Toronto Star, June 27, 2002, p. A28.
27. IBID.
28. IBID.
29. Chantal Hebert, 'Canada's brush with terrorism worth studying', The Toronto Star, June 27, 2002. p. A8.

"I won't hide from you my disappointment. I didn't see the International Criminal Court as a threat to the United States.

There is a certain irony in the fact that the United States, which tends to extraterritorially apply its laws and jurisdiction rather widely, is not willing to participate in a truly international consensus for a court which… would satisfy our requirement for a truly global justice system… It can't be a world where it's always only their justice and their way of applying the rules."

- Canadian Foreign Affairs Minister Bill Graham

Chapter Two

A One-sided Friendship?

Coping with an isolationist America

The U.S. clearly attempts to have its cake and eat it too when it comes to trade on a number of fronts, including softwood lumber, agriculture and natural gas development.

Rather than practice the free, open trade it frequently preaches, the U.S. has instead decided to fully subsidize its overall domestic agricultural production to the maximum extent (and possibly beyond) allowed under World Trade Organization rules.

In early May 2002, Congress approved a bill that increases farmer subsidies by $73.5 billion US. Lyle Vanclief, the U.S. agriculture minister, attacked the move, stating it will severely distort trade, encourage American overproduction, significantly hamper global trade liberalization efforts and make hypocrites of the U.S. 1.

The U.S. has also confirmed duties of 27 per cent against Canadian softwood lumber and has given $10 billion US in loan guarantees to Alaskan gas producers to build a pipeline and not a less expensive alternative that would have involved Canadian gas fields. 2.

In the opinion of Toronto-based author and political commentator Linda McQuaig, "the Chretien government has been capitulating to the Americans almost from the day it took office – but the pace of capitulation has picked up since Sept. 11, 2001." 3.

McQuaig asserts "the Chretien government's acceptance of the North American Free Trade Agreement has stripped us of the power to have an independent industrial or energy policy, if we were ever so inclined." 4.

Toronto Star foreign affairs columnist Gordon Barthos, notes Bush has even rescinded U.S. support of the establishment of an international Criminal Court in the Hague, in the Netherlands, a court that is "designed to end the culture of impunity which allowed a Josef Stalin, a Mao Zedong and a Pol Pot to murder millions in the last century, and evade justice," Barthos chillingly observes. He adds: "Rather than subvert the new court, Americans should embrace it as a guarantor of universal law, and human rights." 5.

Barthos says Bush seems to believe that the new court would hobble American efforts to wage war on deserving foes, when, in fact, the court would still allow Americans accused of war crimes to be tried in the U.S. and would only take on the most serious of cases – and only if the American courts refuse to try them.

As well, Barthos notes Bush's odious American Servicemembers' Protection Act could also easily turn the U.S. into a safe haven for war criminals, because it prevents the world court from extraditing anyone in the U.S.

And it's all just another example of selfish American isolationism.

Barthos objects to "this placing of American interests on a legal pedestal above others," and warns: "Washington can only isolate others with this approach." 6.

Canadian Foreign Affairs Minister Bill Graham roundly condemned the American decision to withdraw from the treaty that created an International Criminal Court. Graham asserted: "I won't hide from you my disappointment. I didn't see the International Criminal Court as a threat to the United States. There is a certain irony in the fact that the United States, which tends to extraterritorially apply its laws and jurisdiction rather widely, is not willing to participate in a truly international consensus for a court which... would satisfy our requirement for a truly global justice system... It can't be a world where it's always only their justice and only their way of applying the rules." 7.

It would seem that to the Americans, there are just two ways of doing things: The American Way and the Wrong Way.

But the rest of the world knows better. Indeed, the Americans still have many lessons to learn from the rest of the world. In a May 2002, live speech on Cuban television to the people of Cuba, former U.S. President Jimmy Carter justly observed: "My nation is hardly perfect in human rights. A very large number of our citizens are in prison, and there is little doubt that the death penalty is imposed most harshly on those who are poor, black, or mentally ill. For more than a quarter-century, we have struggled unsuccessfully to guarantee the basic right of universal health care for our people." 8.

If that message didn't hit home, Bush received a more blunt reminder that the American way isn't necessarily the right way during a state visit he made that same month to Germany.

As the American president arrived in Berlin to promote policies that are unpopular clear across Europe – U.S. trade tariffs, one-sided support for Israel, the portrayal of Iraq as a major threat to the West, rejection of the global warming treaty, rejection of the world court, etc. – he was confronted by thousands of bottle-throwing protestors who had to be contained by tear gas and riot police.

As the Knight Ridder news service noted:

"At a time when Europeans are trying to figure out their place in the world, Bush is widely viewed as a global bully, with little regard for European sensibilities." 9.

Europe's objections with Bush's approach are not surprising. International affairs columnist and political commentator Gwynne Dyer notes the U.S. has engaged in a series of unilateral actions that have served to isolate it from the rest of the world.

As Dyer observes:

"The Bush administration's campaign to free the United States from the constraints imposed by international treaties began with its rejection of the 1997 Kyoto treaty on global climate change. This was followed by U.S. disruptions of a conference aimed at curbing the global trade in small arms, Washington's sabotage of efforts to negotiate enforcement measures for the treaty banning biological weapons, and Bush's December repudiation (with six months notice) of the 1972 Anti-Ballistic Missile treaty." 10.

Dyer also points out that the North Atlantic Treaty Organization – or NATO as it's known to most people – "has grown to include former

Soviet satellites Poland, the Czech Republic and Hungary, and now stands at 19 member nations, a level the U.S. found cumbersome to deal with, which may be why most of consensus-driven NATO was virtually ignored by the U.S. during the War in Afghanistan.

The U.S. instead stuck with a considerably smaller coalition force – including Canada – to fight terrorist groups. " 11.

Yet, the U.S. backed further expansion of NATO to include the addition of three Baltic states in NATO itself and the addition of Russia under the newly approved joint NATO-Russia Council.

Dyer suggests Russia supports this move because it gives that rapidly fading power a bit of lustre and defuses any visible lingering American animosity towards that country.

And the U.S. has its own agenda and its own reasons for supporting NATO expansion.

As Dyer dryly observes: "An expanded NATO promises to paralyse European decision-making utterly." 12.

Dyer explains:

> "The last thing Washington wants is a European superpower challenging its global hegemony. The likelihood that such a power might actually emerge from the current ramshackle process of European 'unification' was always remote, but if you are the reigning global superpower, you can't be too careful about these things." 13.

Political experts such as Dyer suggest that the U.S. is mainly interested in continuing to assert its power and degree of control over the rest of the world, and perhaps expand this reach.

Indeed, I would suggest that the U.S. is the closest thing to an absolute global power that the world has ever seen. And standing up to such a power to express a different point of view or to assert that you're being abused on the trade front is not easy thing to do.

Deputy Prime Minister John Manley asserts that Canada can and does stand up to the United States. Manley says Canada objects to the U.S. decisions to pull out of arms control pacts.

He says Canada has criticized the U.S. on such fronts and also made its views known that it considers Bush's State of the Union Address to have been unnecessarily hard on Iran and North Korea considering both countries are making strides on the diplomatic front to get along with their neighbours and make their societies a little freer. 14.

However, A very different message was also heard the same day Manley made his Feb. 8, 2002 speech, offering assurances of Canada's independent nature.

The Canadian Centre for Policy Alternatives released a report titled 'Lockstep in the Continental Ranks', which warned that Canada is rapidly headed into an increased integration with the United States and appears to be toeing the

American line on most issues while failing to forcefully make its own positions known on trade and other issues of importance to the country. 15.

But Bush's 'my way or the highway' approach to dealing with friends and allies is beginning to wear thin.

As Haroon Siddiqui, the Toronto Star columnist and editorial page editor emeritus, observes:

> "George W. Bush built a quick coalition for the war in Afghanistan, as did his father for the 1991 Gulf War. He is squandering it just as quickly as did the elder Bush. The president's initial measured response to terrorism has given way to a cocky bellicosity that's annoying critics at home, including Bill Clinton, and allies across the Atlantic and beyond.
>
> The European Union and the North Atlantic Treaty Organization have added their collective voices to German, French and even British reservations about his plan to expand the war on terrorism to wherever he sees fit. They are particularly uneasy over his invoking of the anti-terrorism rationale to settle Washington's old scores with Iraq, Iran and North Korea, his so-called "axis of evil." None has been implicated in the Sept. 11 terror." 16.

Siddiqui adds this warning:

> "Bush may also get away with having American soldiers swoop down in dysfunctional Somalia to pluck out alleged Al Qaeda operatives, as Washington has been hinting. But an assault on Iraq, let alone Iran, will be a different matter. It will crack open the fault line between America and Europe, as well as the entire Muslim world, temporarily papered over by the war in Afghanistan." 17.

Canada is clearly in no position to stop the disaster-in-waiting Siddiqui describes.

Nor is our own home and native land free from America's overwhelming push to expand the war on terrorism.

As James Laxer, a York University political science professor notes:

> "The question of the hour for Canadians is how our country will survive the age of imperial America. All the other issues – globalization, the environment, the fate of medicare, control of our fresh water, the struggle for sovereignty in the High Arctic – are subsets of the dominant issue... the United States is the global successor to the British Empire and Imperial Rome. The gap between American military prowess and that of any other power is so huge... The long-term effect of

> Sept. 11 has been to expose to the world an old-fashioned military empire that no longer bothers with the niceties of international covenants. That is the real import of George W. Bush's unveiling of the concept of the "Axis of Evil," the reference to Iraq, Iran and North Korea, in his State of the Union address." 18.

Canada has tried repeatedly to get along with a powerful neighbour that does whatever it wants.

But as Laxer points out, the efforts aren't working:

> "Since Sept. 11, the Chretien government's strategy has been to curry favour with the Americans on border issues, refugee and immigration policy and by participating in America's new war.
>
> Canada's illiberal anti-terrorism law was explicitly drafted with one eye on Washington. And what has been the payoff for all this pandering? Precisely nothing.
>
> On softwood lumber, the U.S. is as implacable as ever. On streamlining commercial traffic across the border, there has been no change..." 19.

From Brian Mulroney on, continentalists – as opposed to nationalists – have dominated Canadian politics, culminating in two free trade agreements with the U.S. and the embracing of the American version of the free market system.

Although the continentalists promised Canadians a cosier relationship with the U.S. would mean greater prosperity for Canadians, Laxer asserts that the decade following the free trade agreements was the worst experienced by Canada since the 1930s Depression:

> "Instead of the stronger, wealthier, more productive country the continentalists promised Canadians, we have become more marginalized and relatively less productive. Putting us in an economic straitjacket where we can no longer fashion government programs to foster the excellence of Canadian companies has been a disaster for Canada. The continentalist cure for the ills they have wrought is to call for yet more integration with the U.S., the scrapping of the loonie and lower taxes that will render our social programs unsustainable." 20.

Laxer says it's time to exercise what clout we do possess: "We will do better with Washington by defining our interests and pursuing them prudently. American companies make billions every year in Canada and we ship more than 50 per cent of our exports to the U.S. That gives us far more freedom to manoeuvre than our timorous elites imagine." 21.

Laxer asserts that we owe it to ourselves to continue to define the Canadian nation and ensure our values survive:

> "History teaches that nations outlive empires… What destroys empires is imperial overstretch, the unwillingness of rulers to understand the limitations of their sway. That is likely the fate of the American Empire in the 21st century.
>
> With judicious realism though, Canada has every prospect of surviving as a country and not merely as a geographical expression." 22.

Richard Gwyn suggests U.S. President George W. Bush simply assumes that the civilized world has bought into his simplistic 'if-you're-not-with-us-you're-against-us' rule and will ultimately support an attack on Iraq.

But Bush is probably correct as only the U.S. has a clear idea of what should be done. Canada and other Western nations are sitting on the fence, asking the U.S. to come up with a case against Iraq. In response, the U.S. can be expected to insist on arms inspections knowing this won't be accepted by Iraq, thereby providing the excuse needed to attack. 23.

Gwyn states Canada needs to emulate America's "quality of conviction," and develop a foreign policy that best reflects our own self interests and capitalizes on our position as a respected middle power that is well-liked around the world:

> "We are relevant internationally only to the extent that we are seen as the good guys. That sounds icky. And it is a bit. But it's a fact. It's why the U.S. wants our approval for its impending attack on Iraq (and also for its controversial anti-missile defence program)… We need a comprehensive foreign policy suited to our national self-interests… increasing our foreign aid, accepting more refugees, making our military into a peacekeeping force, arguing against Washington's treatment of prisoners.
>
> We shouldn't be doing all this only because it is the right thing to do. As much because it's all in our self-interest. Being seen to be doing good defines our distinctiveness… We need to pursue our national self-interest in exactly the same bold and decisive way that Bush is now pursuing the U.S. national interest – but in an entirely different direction because we are an entirely different country." 23.

Gwyn also suggests the U.S. likes going its own way because it can get away with it:

> "If a treaty to ban slavery were proposed in the U.N. today, the U.S. would

> probably reject it as an invasion of its sovereignty. That isn't entirely inconceivable. The U.S. refused to sign the U.N.'s convention on genocide for more than 20 years until the early 1980s, and the Senate then added so many riders that it is effectively inapplicable to whatever the U.S. does… Indeed, splendid isolation, if not isolationism exactly, comes naturally to the U.S. because it is continent sized, in population and resources as well as geography, and so is, or can think of itself as, complete unto itself… As the single superpower, the U.S. doesn't need anyone else and can get away with doing just about anything it wants to do." 24.

In sharp contrast, Canada is a smaller power that relies on co-operation with other nations. Our history is also one of collectivism over individualism and of putting social needs ahead of economic needs.

As Gwyn also notes: "Canadians get involved emotionally in other peoples' problems. We need the world, economically, politically, and culturally. Perhaps our greatest need is psychic. Each time we get involved abroad we send out the message that there are two quite different kinds of people on the North American continent. At least as important, if not a good deal more so, we send that same message right back to ourselves." 25.

Jim Travers, national affairs columnist for The Toronto Star, says the key task now facing Canada's federal government is to "find the fine balance between sharing economic space with a superpower and making the social policy choices that will reinforce the emerging sense of what is important about being Canadian." 26.

Travers also warns:

> "Inevitably, economic decisions, particularly those touching taxation, productivity and competitiveness will shape social programs that are now as much a part of Canada as the maple leaf, the beaver and the sanctity of hockey. What is encouraging is that those critical decisions can be made with the confidence that comes with knowing who we are and what is important." 27.

Linda McQuaig questions why Canada feels it must look to America for a role model and always move in lockstep with the U.S:

"As you may have heard, we must cut taxes and government spending in order to be competitive in the global economy. Just look at the United States; it has low taxes and a competitive economy. But concluding that the U.S. low-tax model is the only one that works in the global economy is like noting the success of Terry Fox and concluding that only one-legged people have the endurance to run long distances." 28.

McQuaig doesn't deny that the U.S. is a competitive country:

> "It's true the U.S. is competitive. The Geneva-based World Economic Forum ranks the United States as one of the most competitive economies in the world. In its most recent annual assessment, it ranks the U.S. Number 2. This is very impressive, almost as impressive as being Number 1 – a spot that is currently held by high-tax Finland… If we insist on imitating a country higher up the competitiveness ladder, why set the bar at Number 2, especially when the Number 1 country (Finland!) offers such perks as a national day care program, free university tuition and five weeks annual paid vacation." 29.

And McQuaig isn't alone among political observers who believe Canada may be better off looking for political and economic answers in Europe than in the United States.

Luke Eric Peterson, an associate of a Geneva-based think tank, suggests Canada should seriously strive to join the European Union, partly because we now have too many trade eggs in the American basket – nearly 90 per cent of exports go south compared with 67 per cent a generation ago – and partly because Canada and Europe share: "liberal attitudes toward soft drugs; stricter controls on guns; abolition of the death penalty; support for publicly funded health care, higher education and public broadcasting; and adherence to a range of multilateral covenants including one to create an International Criminal Court." 30.

Given our extremely high percentage of trade with the U.S., it's little wonder that our economy is hurt every time the Americans decide – however unfairly – to slap a duty on our softwood lumber or other exports.

As Peterson points out, our country is "worryingly overexposed to the U.S. market… as a consequence, Canada's manoeuvring room on many political issues has become pathetically circumscribed." 31.

Peterson objects that instead of Canada forging closer ties with Europe – the world's second-largest economy and our second-largest trading partner – we seem determined to get cosier still with the American elephant:

> "In recent weeks, the policy options for our supplicant economy have been carefully laid out by our captains of industry and their indentured think tanks, consisting largely of varying degrees of "deeper integration" with the U.S. economy. If you get bucked off the U.S. bronco, so the thinking goes, simply lash yourself to it more tightly next time. Never mind if you cut off circulation to your own brain in the process." 32.

Peterson says joining the Europeans would be healthy for Canada's psyche which always seems depressed even when repeatedly told by the U.N. Canada is the best place in the world to live: "Perhaps if Canada were part of a larger political community, we might cease to glance nervously over our shoulder, and perhaps, one day, even come to admire our own reflection in the mirror. By stiffening Canada's backbone, membership in the European Union might preserve our nation's fraying sovereignty – rather than simply see ever greater swaths of it surrendered to a single self-absorbed trading partner." 33.

Canada's closeness to the American border will always ensure our two nations continue to trade and will remain major trading partners. Peterson accepts that but points out:

> "The more important question, however, is whether Canada's vision of itself as a society might be preserved though marriage into a like-minded political family. The alternative is clear enough: a loveless wedding with the U.S., precipitated by shotgun-toting customs guards." 34.

As Peterson concludes: "Given America's general indifference to our nation, one wonders, if Canada were to run off and elope with Europe – but leave the gas and oil flowing – would the elephant even notice that its bed had grown slightly colder?" 35.

But why leave the gas flowing? As The Toronto Star states in an editorial: "U.S. President George W. Bush is no free trader. He allowed the U.S. lumber industry to level the same trumped-up charges against Canadian softwood producers that international tribunals repeatedly dismissed... He has failed to stand up to protectionists in Congress who are proposing massive new agricultural subsidies, while threatening to impose tariffs on Canadian wheat." 36.

Noting that there is "one important difference, however, between Canada and other countries that the U.S. has hurt – we signed a free trade agreement with Washington," the Star concludes the U.S. isn't trading freely or fairly with Canada and suggests the drastic measure of cutting off the flow of gas: "At this point, the only option open to us is to demonstrate to the Americans that free trade is a two-way street by linking softwood directly to their thirst for our energy supplies. Ottawa has repeatedly refused to make this link. But to do nothing is to invite even more U.S. abuse." 37.

Gord McNulty, an editorial writer with The Hamilton Spectator, also expresses alarm over Canada's "deteriorating trade relationship." 38.

As McNulty notes:

> "For someone who is supposed to be a leading advocate of free trade, George W. Bush has an odd way of showing it. Bush is proving to be a champion of

> protectionism who wields a big stick at Canada's expense… The hypocrisy in Washington is amazing. The Bush administration, often critical of European Union agricultural subsidies, is defending the same policies it has condemned. So much for the reality that subsidies will promote U.S. overproduction, distort trade by closing markets to Canadian farmers, and undermine freer global trade." 39.

Noting the North American Free Trade Agreement dispute settlement mechanisms and the World Trade Organization remedies are time-consuming and uncertain, McNulty also urges Canada to "say no to the American desire for access to Canada's energy… An aggressive Canadian stance on energy would be a wakeup cal for Bush. Given the beating that Canada is absorbing from this president, Chretien may not have a better option." 40.

Such calls for alarm underline the grave situation Canada is in: Our nation depends more than ever on U.S. trade for our standard of living.

As our dependency has grown – nearly 90 per cent of our exports now go to the U.S., up from 67 per cent a generation ago – the U.S. has grown more powerful, more belligerent and protectionist, even though Canada has long been, without question, America's best friend and biggest trading partner.

David Crane says Canada faces a serious internal threat from business leaders pushing for deep integration with the U.S.

As Crane warns:

"Deep integration means, in reality, subjugating many of Canada's policies to those of the U.S. – including trade, immigration, energy, water, our dollar, taxation, defence and the environment. However, it won't gain any corresponding voice in the U.S. government where decisions affecting many aspects of Canadian life would be made. In effect, Canada could become another Puerto Rico, subject to many policies of the U.S., but without a serious political voice in those decisions. 41.

Noting "the United States is instinctively unilateral in its approach," Crane cautions:

> "The U.S. imperial superpower, acts on the basis of economic and military power, not shared decision-making, and, given the country's great size, would not consider serious sharing of decisions and power with a much smaller country... Canadians would not only be almost powerless in addressing fundamental future economic concerns, but would also lose the capacity to control the social environment and the ability to adjust to change because social policy would also end up being driven by U.S. policies." 42.

Peter McKenna and Reginald C. Stuart, who both teach history and politics at Mount Saint Vincent University in Halifax, concur that talk of establishing a government-appointed task force to study U.S.-Canada relations is a waste of time, as "the thrust of Canada's difficulties vis-à-vis Washington are well known. It begins and ends with what the late Speaker of the House of Representatives, Tip O'Neill, said prophetically: "All politics is local." It follows that Canada only raises eyebrows on Capital Hill when it impinges on localized political matters, such as trade, water diversions and border security." 43.

McKenna and Stuart suggest the situation is unlikely to change: "The fact of the matter is that since we don't vote in U.S. elections, domestic political considerations are always going to trump our interests." 44.

Richard Gwyn asserts getting cozy with the U.S. doesn't work. He notes the late Prime Minister Pierre Trudeau was sharply critical of the U.S. – and the U.S. still brought us into the exclusive G7 club of nations. In contrast, Alberta is slavishly pro-American but it's also the most damaged by U.S. trade policies on lumber, beef, agriculture, and energy beef. Sucking up to the U.S. achieves nothing. 45.

Gwyn says the reason sucking up, or not, makes little difference has everything to do with the fact that the "defining rule in the U.S. is that 'All politics is local.' Congress, egged on by the lobbyists, isn't out to get British steelmakers or Canadian lumber companies because they're mad at Ottawa or Westminster over some... policy issue. They're out to get the votes of their constituents by protecting their jobs or by shoving money at them. This system is extremely annoying for outsiders." 46.

Linda McQuaig notes former Prime Minister Brian Mulroney loved sucking up to former U.S. President Ronal Reagan, even to the extent of signing a free trade agreement in the 1980s that failed to guarantee access to the American market (Canada's sole reason for negotiating such a deal in the first place).

As McQuaig notes: "When Simon Reisman, our chief negotiator, finally realized the U.S. wouldn't budge on the guaranteed access issue, he... told Mulroney he couldn't get a deal worth signing. Ignoring Reisman's advice, Mulroney signed a deal anyway." 47.

Canadian Foreign Affairs Minister Bill Graham notes Canada stood by the U.S., its closest ally, in the months following the September 11, 2001 atrocities but now needs to assert itself and criticize the United States for throwing its weight around on the world stage. "Immediately after Sept. 11 there was a natural, tremendous rallying around the United States," Graham told The Toronto Star's Allan Thompson, "but we've always said: 'We stand beside you, but we don't jump how high you tell us to jump." 48.

As Thompson reports: "Graham noted there is now a "degree of angst and irritation," about recent U.S. actions. He cited the farm bill that dramatically increased subsidies to American farmers, trade barriers in steel and softwood lumber that defy the U.S. credo on free trade and Washington's withdrawal from the International Criminal Court and the Kyoto climate change accord." 49.

Avrum D. Lank, a columnist for the Milwaukee Journal Sentinel says Bush's free trade message is steeped in hypocrisy: "When it comes to free trade, U.S. President George Bush is two-faced, unwilling to exert the type of focused consistent political leadership he has demonstrated in the war against terrorism…" 50.

Lank says that on the subject of opening up markets at home and abroad to free and fair trade, Bush is talking out of both sides of his mouth: "To the world he has sent one message; to political backers in the United States, another. His message to the world has been consistent and laudable: Free trade is an unalloyed good that leads to the enrichment of all involved. It is something to be pursued for its own sake, even if in the short run it hurts segments of a nation's economy." Unfortunately, Bush has, as Lank quite correctly observes "weakened his hand by agreeing to exempt large segments of the U.S. economy from the less fortunate short-term outcomes of free trade." 51.

By essentially exempting the American steel industry through the imposition of tariffs against steel imported from a number of other countries, Bush has simply propped up some globally inefficient and uncompetitive American steel mills while infuriating the rest of world by preaching a free trade gospel he doesn't follow.

The softwood lumber duties and the $180-billion farm subsidy for wealthy American farmers and ranchers simply underlined the message that Bush doesn't practice what he preaches.

All of this leads Lank to question: "How with a straight face can Bush ask Japan to open its rice market or the European Union to stop subsidizing its picturesque countryside if he is willing to send pitchforks full of U.S. tax dollars to the farmers of Texas, South Dakota and Wisconsin? How can he negotiate free trade in the Western Hemisphere under a fast-track arrangement with the United States closing its domestic markets to foreign steel?" 52.

Lank then answers his own questions by observing: "Bush has taken these contradictory stands for a reason as old as the nation – domestic politics… Free trade might be fine in theory, but in the mind of George W. Bush it counts as nothing when balanced against electoral votes." 53.

Lank concludes: "One thing is certain: If a foreign nation pursued the Janus-faced trade policies coming out of his administration, George W. Bush would yell foul." 54.

McKenna and Stuart assert that rather than waste more time with a task force on bilateral relations, Canada needs to take a different approach: "We need to consider the following questions: How does Canada penetrate the U.S. bureaucratic labyrinth, secure a place on the congressional radar screen or get its calls put through the White House switchboard? What measures or strategies can Canada adopt to ensure that its interests are advanced and protected? Canada needs to be more proactive in its relations with the U.S., and much quicker off the mark with frank and intelligent policy recommendations. By way of illustration, Ottawa was successful in getting in on the ground floor with respect to border security – which culminated in a comprehensive and mutually satisfactory 30-point "Smart Border" plan." 55.

Paul Krugman, a columnist for The New York Times, notes U.S. President George Bush preaches free trade "but has turned out to be quite a protectionist."

As Krugman observes: "The steel tariff and farm bill attracted the most attention, but they are part of a broader picture that includes the punitive (and almost completely unjustified) tariff on Canadian softwood lumber… When it comes to free trade, the Bush administration is all for it – unless there is some political cost, however small, to honouring its alleged principles." Krugman notes in sharp contrast to Bush, former President

Bill Clinton took political risks and reached across party lines to gain support for NAFTA. Krugman adds: "If Bill Clinton had given the steel industry the tariffs it wanted, Al Gore would probably be living in the White House. But administration officials actually worried about consequences – for the nation, and for the world economy – of giving in to special interests." 56.

Toronto Star writer Thomas Walkom suggests Bush is simply milking the War on Terrorism for all its worth, using world sympathy for New York victims to push selfish goals: "Even beyond oil, the attacks on New York and Washington opened up possibilities for a president whose very legitimacy was under question until Sept. 11. In effect, they gave him and his administration carte blanche… Does the president want to settle scores with Iraq, the enemy his father never quite beat? No problem. All he has to do is mention the T-word and Congress falls into line… If during these grand adventures, the Bush warriors happen to run across terrorists, well, that's fine too. But it's clearly not a priority." 57.

Walkom may be stretching things a bit with an assessment that's overly harsh on Bush.

But unfortunately, we have the same George W. Bush now that we had prior to Sept. 11, 2001: A president who is clearly in over his head, who has no idea how to negotiate mutually agreeable understandings with other nations, who has no sense of diplomacy, who throws trade penalties at innocent countries that produce better goods and services than those American firms screaming for protectionism. Most incredibly, Bush has no problem in demanding the help of those same nations he's unfairly hammering – or Bushwhacking – with trade penalties.

Given the awesome military might of the United States, Bush's lack of experience on the world stage is clearly a troublesome issue that isn't going to go away anytime soon. Bush is virtually alone among free world leaders in his easy willingness to use military power to get his way, however flimsy the case for war.

This second choice for U.S. president is clearly no statesman: Bullying abroad is no way to build up credibility at home. It's certainly no way to earn the confidence of other nations. One can only imagine what other world leaders think of his simplistic world views and his knee-jerk willingness to pull out of pacts solely because these deals – like all deals – have flaws.

The fact that Bush pulls out of treaties, but offers nothing in the way of alternatives, only points up his severe lack of statesmanship.

It's not that he's a bad guy at heart: I don't believe Bush necessarily sets out to be cruel or callous to other nations. But his tendency to focus myopically on American interests to the exclusion of the interests of other nations, to the exclusion of what is actually fair for all parties, is an ongoing worry.

He's a champion of free trade – until some domestic votes are at stake, at which point he'll put communist countries to shame with his generous trade-distorting subsidies for domestic industries.

Given all of this, Canada needs to find new coping mechanisms that go beyond appealing to our erratic friend's good side.

We should consider tying the U.S. need for our energy resources to Free Trade amendments that will exclude Canada from trade penalties unless there is undeniable evidence of unfair trade.

Included in this approach would be recognition that the Canadian way of doing things – such as charging low fees to log Crown lands – isn't wrong, it's just slightly different than the American way and deserves respect.

We should also pursue expansion of trade with other nations – whether we join a European Union model or not – as it's simply not wise to keep all of your trade eggs in one basket.

And we need to lend our advice to our American friend and strive to work out long-term solutions to our differences.

Otherwise, when we least expect it… we'll get Bushwhacked again.

End Notes

1. CP, 'U.S. takes a hard line over trade', The Toronto Star, May 4, 2002, pg. A22.
2. IBID.
3. Linda McQuaig, 'U.S. likely to stonewall probe by Baril', TO Star, May 19/2002 A15
4. IBID.
5. Gordon Barthos, 'America plays global scofflaw', Toronto Star, May 16/2002, A28.
6. IBID.
7. Tim Harper, 'Graham rips U.S. decision on world court', TO Star, May 7, 2002. A6.
8. Jimmy Carter live speech, Cuba, May 12/02
9. Daniel Rubin and Ron Hutcheson, 'Bush's tour start in Berlin sparks demonstrations', Knight Ridder Newspapers, as carried by The Hamilton Spectator, May 23, 2002, B2.
10. Gwynne Dyer, 'The world didn't change that much on Sept. 11. The attacks had far-reaching effects but other events were just as significant', The Hamilton Spectator, Pg. D2, January 3, 2002.
11. Gwynne Dyer, 'Expanded NATO will paralyse Europe', The Hamilton Spectator, May 29, 2002. Pg. C2.
12. IBID.
13. IBID.
14. Allan Thompson, 'Canada is able to stand up to U.S: Manley, TO Star, Feb. 9, 2002.
15. IBID.
16. Haroon Siddiqui, 'Bellicose Bush pushing his luck with coalition', The Toronto Star, pg. A13, Feb. 10, 2002.

17. IBID.
18. James Laxer, 'Surviving American Imperialism, The Toronto Star, pg. A13, Feb. 17, 2002.
19. IBID.
20. IBID.
21. IBID.
22. Richard Gwyn, 'Self-interest should guide foreign policy', The Toronto Star, Feb. 20, 2002, pg. A21.
23. IBID.
24. IBID.
25. IBID.
26. Jim Travers, 'What Uncle Sam wants isn't us', The Toronto Star, May 25, 2002, G2.
27. IBID.
28. Linda McQuaig, 'Bold Harris helped cause of the rich and powerful', The Toronto Star, May 26, 2002. Pg. A15.
29. IBID.
30. Luke Eric Peterson, 'We might be better off with Europe', TO Star, May 22, 2002. A26.
31. IBID.
32. IBID.
33. IBID.
34. IBID.
35. IBID.
36. The Toronto Star, editorial, 'No wood, no gas', The Toronto Star, May 6, 2002. A22.
37. IBID.
38. Gord McNulty, 'Trade wars: Play the energy card. It's time for Chretien to get tough with U.S., The Hamilton Spectator, May 7, 2002. Pg. A10.
39. IBID.

40. IBID.
41. David Crane, 'Beware this phrase: 'Deep integration', The Hamilton Spectator, May 7, 2002. Pg. B4.
42. IBID.
43. Peter McKenna and Reginald C. Stuart, 'Guiding Canada-U.S. relations', The Toronto Star, June 17, 2002. P. A19.
44. IBID.
45. Richard Gwyn, 'Fishing in troubled waters', The Toronto Star, June 2, 2002. Pg. A13.
46. IBID.
47. Linda McQuaig, 'Alliance leader seems to believe Canadians are second-rate', The Toronto Star, June 2, 2002. Pg. A13.
48. Allan Thompson, 'Graham keen to take on U.S.', The Toronto Star, June 10, 2002. A7.
49. IBID.
50. Avrum D. Lank, 'Bush's double standards', Milwaukee Journal Sentinel, May16/02 A26
51. IBID.
52. IBID.
53. IBID.
54. IBID.
55. Peter McKenna and Reginald C. Stuart, 'Guiding Canada-U.S. relations', The Toronto Star, June 17, 2002. P. A19.
56. Paul Krugman, Catering to special interests' The Toronto Star, June 17, 2002. p. A20.
57. Thomas Walkom, 'War on terror little to do with terror', The Toronto Star, June 18, 2002. p. A25.

Part Two

Other Post Cold War Dilemmas

Russia's fragile democracy is often cited by the masses as a scapegoat for economic failings.

The country's fellow ex-Soviet member states want little to do with the former imperial Russians.

The economy is struggling and most Russians live in poverty.

And so, the question remains:
Can Russia survive the collapse of the USSR?

Chapter Three

New Russia

Old problems

Exploring the Post-USSR Security Dilemma

Russia's cosier relationship with the American superpower, post 9-11, is a recent phenomena that may not outlive the animosities of the past. Even now, many are questioning Russia's re-labelling of Chechnya rebels as "terrorists."

And Russia's economic instability and shaky democracy have risen as major concerns since the Cold War ended a dozen years ago.

Let's take an insightful trip back in time.

In 1989, the Berlin Wall came crashing down, taking the Cold War and East European communism with it. As political security expert Thomas Risse-Kappen notes, this dramatic change also meant "the bipolar order, which allegedly preserved the peace in Europe for more than forty years by dividing the continent and freezing the social and political structures, collapsed within a couple of months." 1.

Noting that the former Soviet Union's "economic burden of sustaining an empire, and maintaining a huge military establishment was crushing," veteran political observer William Hyland asserts "by the time Brezhnev died... the economy of the Soviet Union was bankrupt, its ideology sterile and its policies impotent." 2.

The USSR presidency of Mikhail Gorbachev, in the mid-to-late 1980s, sought to counter political inertia and economic decline. Hyland notes Gorbachev "acted to save the Bolshevik revolution by radical economic reforms, political liberalization, and, finally, a new foreign policy. He thus became the crucial figure in ending the cold war." 3.

The Gorbachev reforms unleashed long-suppressed desires for political and economic freedom as glasnost - or openness - exposed corruption, bureaucratic incompetence and organized crime. Soviet flaws were unveiled and nationalistic forces to emerge - especially in Russia. Political commentator Walter Laqueur notes, "As Marxism-Leninism was tried and found wanting, 'Westernism' became the main culprit, and internationalism gave way to a new wave of Russian patriotism." 4.

Inevitably, the very high, unattainable expectations held out for democracy in Russia would result in widespread cynicism by the masses and the return of an unhealthy hyper nationalism which reopened old ethnic wounds.

As political observer Martin Crouch points out, the unintended effect of the Gorbachev initiatives "may well have been to exacerbate inter-ethnic rivalries," while his perestroika and glasnost initiatives "almost certainly heightened expectations while not necessarily providing adequate justification for... inequalities." 5.

But there was now no turning back. As Bohdan Nahaylo and Victor Swoboda adroitly suggest, "inadvertently, by loosening controls in order to facilitate economic modernization, Gorbachev let the genie out of the bottle." 6.

Change became unstoppable. The Economist asserts Gorbachev's "greatness lay in his capacity to destroy everything he tried to save – his party's monopoly on power, its ideology and its empire." 7.

The USSR disintegrated and, as Hyland reminds us, "the Red Army began to go home," starting the Czechoslovakia on February 26, 1990. Hyland notes that the Warsaw Pact was by then "almost an empty shell, and it was formally dissolved in March 1991." 8.

This was a dramatic end to the 73-year legacy of communism, which followed the 1917 Russian Revolution.

As Walter LaFeber recounts, this legacy began when "Vladimir Lenin's Bolshevik movement used the devastation, chaos, and poverty caused by World War I to overthrow the Russian government and establish a Soviet."

All of this meant, "the ever-expanding czarist empire now possessed an ideological force, Marxism, supposedly driven by historical law and dedicated to world revolution." 9.

Of course, communism would prove far less successful than capitalism and democracy. By hypocritically rewarding a favoured few and then subjecting the masses to one-size-fits-all mediocre compensation regardless of the value of their work, communism removed any real incentive for anyone to excel at anything. Why become a dedicated doctor or scientist at all when a hack or an unskilled party member is paid as much or more? Renowned political commentator Zbiginiew Brzezinski asserts, "communism will be remembered largely as the twentieth century's most extraordinary political and intellectual aberration." 10.

Yet, any cause for celebration in the wake of USSR communism's collapse has been tempered by the uncertain peace, which has followed. The main source of this uncertainty is Russia, long the centre of a great empire, but now a deeply troubled, quasi-democratic world power wracked by hyper nationalism and a crumbling economy.

Russia also faces several potential security threats, the largest of which is internal in the form of an unstable political system, unstable economy and fragile democracy.

Of external security concerns, Ukraine has

emerged as the principal source of anxiety while other neighbouring states add their own dimensions of uncertainty to a volatile international security mix.

But at the core of Russian woes is Russia's unenviable juxtaposition of a failing economy wed to a shaky emerging democratic structure combined with continued, if declining, military power and latent desires to play a larger role on the world stage.

For all of these reasons, I would set Russia's place on the security continuum as being well past the point of 'No cause for concern' and approaching 'Extreme cause for concern'.

Underpinning this chapter's rationale for placing Russia in the final quadrant for security risk is that nation's weak, unstable economy. The Economist noted that in 1991, when the Soviet Union completely collapsed and Russia elected Boris Yeltsin president, "the economy they inherited was barely a going concern... the shops were empty and there appeared real danger of widespread hunger in big cities." 11.

The Economist notes Russia initially lowered inflation but was soon again gripped by an outbreak of hyperinflation due to politically-popular yet unhealthy economic bail-outs of entirely uncompetitive, lethargic, state-owned manufacturers which responded to change by doing nothing and "went on producing goods for which there was no demand..." 12.

Asserting that state subsidies are "particularly mad because Russia is already over-industrialized," The Economist suggests that "Russia would be better off if much of its heavy industry went bankrupt and workers and capital were deployed elsewhere," as the country's output has "fallen more in the past three years than America's did during the Great Depression." 13.

The Economist also asserts that Russian claims of fewer than 1 million unemployed are fiction as a survey of more than 700 Russian factories showed many are at least 20 per cent overstaffed and prone to putting workers on unpaid leave. Unfortunately, however, "for those without jobs, absolute poverty threatens... unemployment benefits are... a third of the official subsistence level..." 14.

As well, Boris Fedorov, former Russian finance minister, notes that a grossly inefficient monopoly governs the production and price of bread, relying on subsidies every step of the way, from collective farms to grain elevators and bakers. Fedorov suggests that this system is so inefficient that "it would probably be cheaper for us to buy grain from Canada and there would be less corruption." 15.

Meanwhile, Russian GDP fell 38 per cent from 1990-1993 and although very recent statistics are not available, there is no reason to expect any significant improvement. As well, unemployment could soon exceed 10 million people or about 14 per cent of the workforce, a higher level than any other large European country with the exception of Spain. 16.

Brzezinski notes that compounding the problems of Russia's frail economy, are several factors, including the sad facts that "the Great Russian homeland lacks commercial outlets to the world's oceans, adequate arable land, and natural resources."

He states Russia is "also cursed by an inhospitable climate and lacks clearly defined natural or ethnic boundaries," opening the "mind-boggling prospect of an impoverished Russia still having to one day accommodate many millions of Great Russian expellees from the non-Russian lands." 17.

Although economic reforms are blamed in Russia for massive social upheaval, increased unemployment and higher levels of poverty, The Economist suggests the real problem is that reforms are not proceeding quickly enough, leaving the inescapable upheaval to linger.

The Russian people have not embraced the market economy. The Economist concludes: "If liberal capitalism is to continue advancing, it must overcome the entrenched scepticism of the people that it benefits." 18.

The Economist notes that Russia's anti-reform political parties have tried to capitalize on economic hardships by presenting the struggling economy as a victim of reform. 19.

Indeed. In Russia, a country in which democracy is an untested experiment, politics can take a decidedly bizarre turn. In August 1993, Alexander Rutskoi, a would-be rival to president Boris Yeltsin, staged an armed insurrection and captured the Russian parliament.

The Economist notes, "Yeltsin had to choose between smashing his rival with force or else seeing himself, his government and any real prospect of reform destroyed." Yeltsin used tank shelling to recapture and recover Russia's parliament. The Economist notes: "The threat, in the end, was extreme – and so, necessarily, was the response." 20.

However, one of the most disturbing repercussions of the recapture of parliament was that Yeltsin, in sending in the tanks, put the generals in the realm of politics.

Asserting that "the army is already too influential in Russia's foreign policy," The Economist notes the army is indeed very much "behind Russia's increasing readiness to throw its weight around in the rest of the former Soviet Union – the flash of gold braid is discernible in warnings to Poland and other ex-members of the ex-Warsaw Pact not to join NATO..." 21.

As political observer Malcolm Gray points out, the 1993 tanks incident revealed disturbing instability and unpredictability in Russian politics and left the West worrying about Yeltsin's hold on power. 22.

One should also consider that organized crime on an almost unimaginable scale has created severe domestic problems within Russia and is making the nation's transition to a market economy a harsh nightmare. Izvestia reports that "between 70% and 80% of all privatized enterprises and commercial banks have had extortion payments exacted... the amount of the tribute ranges from 10% to 20% of turnover, which frequently comes to over half of an enterprise's gross profits." 23.

Izvestia adds that highly-organized gangs, with dossiers on prominent politicians, have worked their way into the political system, have confiscated cars from ordinary citizens, have turned restaurants into their own private clubs and have exacted tribute from gardeners, private farmers, gardeners and residents of Kazan, Moscow and St. Petersburg.

Izvestia warns that "failure to take resolute measures to remove the economic roots of crime and to provide legal guarantees for the struggle against organized crime, as well as a lack of political will in combating organized crime, could bring the national-socialists to power... " 24.

This leads us to consider the threat posed by the national-socialist party led by hate-mongering Vladimir Zhirinovsky. While Zhirinovsky has not yet achieved power, the threat remains that he one day may. He first gained international attention in the early 1990s when he emerged as a serious contender for political power. As The Economist noted, Zhirinovsky's "gruesomely misnamed" neo-fascist Liberal Democrats won one-fifth of votes cast and a fifth of the 225 seats in the State Duma (the Russian parliament's lower house). Zhirinovsky was also by that point campaigning for the 1996 presidency and exploiting unrest over economic reforms, which unavoidably mean business bankruptcies and strict budgets to curb inflation. The threat was very real. As The Economist ominously added: "The two great enemies of liberal democracy in the 20th century have been communism and fascism. Russia, having rid itself of the former is now flirting with the latter." 25.

The Economist also sees a parallel between modern day Russia and Nazi Germany, which "serves as a reminder of how vulnerable democracy can be if national pride and living standards are simultaneously slashed."

Noting that the example of Germany "suggests that even a minority of voters can lay the foundations for fascism," The Economist then soundly points out that "a larger share of Russian voters... chose a party that has in common with fascism a virulent form of nationalism, a militarist streak, anti-Semitism and a belief in the corporate state." 26.

Although Russian President Vladimir Putin, a moderate, is in power now, such an outcome was far from certain back in the early

1990s. In fact, The Economist expressed grave concerns Zhirinovsky could topple Yeltsin, "unless Mr. Yeltsin is careful to build up coalitions to support his policies. If he were to fail and the confrontation turned nasty, as the last one did, Mr. Yeltsin could not rely on the support of the army which voted heavily for Mr. Zhirinovsky." [27]

As The Economist also observes, "Mr. Zhirinovsky denies that he is a fascist but his party espouses policies of xenophobia, anti-Semitism, militarism and corporatism that seem strikingly fascist." Indeed, Liberal Democrats pledged to "stop all aid to the former republics of the Soviet Union; to stop the conversion of arms factories and to export weapons to anyone who can afford them." [28]

Zhirinovsky's published comments advocate war to revive the Russian army. He would expel up to a million Azeris from Russia, and "if a German looks at Russia the wrong way when I'm in the Kremlin, you Germans will pay for all we Russians built up in Germany." [29]

Zhirinovsky also harbours hatred towards Japan: "I would bomb the Japanese. I would sail our large navy around their small island and if they so much as cheeped, I would nuke them." [30]

Oddly observing, "Sometimes Russia has been overwhelmed by anti-Semitism," he adds, "This phenomenon was provoked only by the Jews themselves." [31]

Political analyst Michael McFaul notes

other political observers had been too quick to denounce Vladimir Zhirinovsky as merely "a kook, a clown, someone who does not even fully believe what he says." Yet, as McFaul concludes, based on Zhironovsky's popular support, it's clear such assumptions "spring from wishful, not critical thinking." 32.

Writing in 1993, McFaul warned that:

> "We deploy high liberal hopes against the hard reality of Russia's volatile and precarious political situation, filtering in only the truth that we want to hear... the factors that propelled Zhirinovsky's protest victory …are likely to intensify… With higher government spending on inefficient industries and hyperinflation now likely, the economy will further tilt Russian politics in favour of extremism." 33.

McFaul points out that "Zhirinovsky's agenda was clear, if somewhat polemical during the 1990 campaign: he wants to make Russia great again." McFaul also adds that "while Russia's Choice told people to prepare for more sacrifice, Zhirinovsky retorted that Russians had suffered enough, first under seventy years of communism and then under two years of "shock therapy" imposed by the "imperialism" of the International Monetary Fund and the World Bank." 34.

Zhirinovsky, observes McFaul, has "vowed to use the Russian army to enrich the country, be it against Azeris in Russia's farmer markets, Jews in Moscow's banks, Ukrainians in Ukraine (a country that Zhirinovsky does not recognize) or Americans in Alaska." 35.

McFaul warned against underestimating Zhirinovsky, who received 6 million votes in the 1990 election. Zhirinovsky could, once in power, use the Russian Constitution to "help consolidate a fascist dictatorship."

McFaul adds that even if Zhirinovsky himself self-destructs; there are other fascists, including Nikolai Lysenko, who are actively building popular support of their own. 36.

Political observer Paul Quinn-Judge observes that "in a striking echo of the writings of Hitler, Zhirinovsky complains of a bad childhood and claims his deprivation and isolation forced him to concentrate on the one overriding idea of his political philosophy: "the last surge south," the expansion of Russia, by force of arms, back across the newly independent republics of the former USSR, through Turkey, Iran and Afghanistan, to the shores of the Indian Ocean." 37.

Quinn-Judge notes Zhirinovsky "reserves special venom for peoples from the southern fringe of the former USSR. 'Like cockroaches' he says, southerners have "already spread beyond the Urals... All our problems come from the south... Nothing would happen to the world even if the whole Turkish nation perished." 38.

The Economist, in 1993, ominously warned that "Zhirinovsky's success may well strengthen the hand of neo-fascists in Ukraine… a like success by them would bring closer the threat of Russo-Ukrainian war." 39.

Zhirinovsky's threats to other nations must be taken seriously as they flow from a politician with growing popular support and whose views reflect a growing willingness among Russians to restore a sense of empire.

Brzezinski argues that the outcome of the Russian election and Zhirinovsky's gains are evidence of a popular "protest against Russia's loss of status in the world."

Brzezinski further argues that Russia is already behaving oppressively towards the ex-Soviet republics and may seek to regain some semblance of empire by subordinating Ukraine. He asserts the response from the West should be to keep Russia out of NATO but let the Czech Republic, Hungary and Poland in while promoting consolidation of the independence of the other states. 40.

Hyland feels that "it is difficult to believe that Russia will remain a second-rate power. Inevitably a Soviet-Russian state will revive, whether as a liberal social democracy, an enlightened despotism or a brutal dictatorship... it will want a large military establishment, almost certainly larger than other powers will believe justified." 41.

Thoughts of a militarily strong Russia with fascist elements taking power understandably have neighbours on edge. Ronald Asmus, Richard Kugler and Stephen Larrabee note security vulnerability of Eastern European states is made more threatening by the existence of "strong residual fears about the threat of a possibly resurgent Russia – a nation that has demonstrated real signs of instability, potential for a shift to the right and flirtations with imperial restoration." 42.

That instability, combined with the popularity of fascists such as Zhirinovsky, have given Russia a security dilemma in which even a modest arms build-up may be construed by neighbouring states as evidence of something far more sinister. The situation is made still more complicated by the insistence of Russian fascists that neighbouring states should be dealt with harshly for alleged mistreatment of ethnic Russian minorities. As Brzezinski notes:

> "Representing a potential time bomb for truly violent national feuding is the fact that about 25 million Great Russians live scattered among the non-Russians, and more than 40 million non-Russians live outside their ethnic territories... these 'outsiders' who number more than 65 million combined, represent the potential precipitating cause, as well as the likely victims, of any large-scale national strife." 43.

Armed conflict has also been made more likely with the loss of an East European security structure after the collapse of the Warsaw Pact. Asmus, Kugler and Larrabee suggest, "Events in former Yugoslavia underscore how war is far more likely in the absence of a functioning security structure." 44.

Asserting that "immense problems facing the new democracies in the East are increasingly compounded by political gridlock, economic recession and resurgent nationalism," Asmus, Kugler and Larrabee describe "an eastern arc" of instability "running between Germany and Russia from northern Europe down through Turkey, the Caucasus and middle Asia," in which "the Soviet collapse has left behind significant and unbalanced military forces and weapons inventories among nations experiencing a wave of instability and conflict generated by virulent nationalism." 45.

Suggesting that East-Central Europe is "littered with potential mini-Weimar Republics, each capable of inflicting immense violence on the others," Asmus, Kugler and Larrabee add "paradoxically, while heavily armed, these countries nonetheless lack the ability to defend themselves against major outside aggressors."

The trio further suggests that such eastern arc conflicts can thus be deemed "increasingly generated by antidemocratic and anti-Western ideologies that threaten the liberal-democratic foundations of Western Europe and the nascent democracies of the former Soviet bloc." 46.

Our trio of experts also observe that in Eastern Europe, local conflicts always carry the potential of escalating into regional wars risking the involvement of major powers such as Russia while an accompanying "spillover, in the form of political and economic instability and refugees is a real danger." 47.

Asmus, Kugler and Larrabee further note Ukraine offers a potentially stabilizing presence because it "acts as an important strategic buffer between Europe and Russia," and in light of the uncertainties surrounding Russian democracy, Ukraine "represents the best guarantee against Russian imperial restoration from the point of view of Eastern Europe, especially of Poland." 48.

Unfortunately, Ukraine is currently anything but stable and instead represents a source of conflict with Russia because neither nuclear power trusts the other and both risk sliding into a severely troublesome security dilemma in which either side could misread the others signals and make an extreme response.

Writing in the early 1990s, political observer Richard Betts underlined the potential for Russian-Ukrainian conflict when he noted that "one nightmare would be a Russian attack on Ukraine – far less fanciful than a Soviet attack on NATO ever was: Russian vice-president Rutskoi has already broached the issue of recovering the Crimea for Russia." 49.

Yet, Betts also notes the West is unlikely to include Ukraine in a security umbrella such as NATO as "under true collective security, members of the system would have to aid Ukraine – doing what NATO would not do for Hungary in 1956 – thus evoking the danger of escalation and nuclear war." Betts chillingly concludes "under realist norms, the West should leave Ukraine to its fate – tragic for the Ukrainians, but safer for everyone else." 50.

The Economist similarly suggests the West would take a hands-off approach to Ukraine and not engage in any form of risky intervention: "The West is not inclined to help. Ukraine has hyperinflation, and its Russian-speaking south and east show signs of wanting to secede. Should Ukraine turn into a second Yugoslavia – or worse, find itself at war with Russia over some territorial dispute (Crimea, say) – America and its allies would want to stay clear." 51.

The likely hands-off approach of the West is not without risks of its own.

On this, Asmus, Kugler and Larrabee urge: "The West should strongly resist any Russian effort to reincorporate Ukraine. If it does not, Ukraine will be driven in a more nationalist direction and toward the retention of nuclear weapons. The West should also encourage Ukraine's Europeanization, its development of closer ties to Central Europe... thereby reducing prospects for the emergence of a nationalistic, xenophobic regime that could threaten neighbours, especially Poland." [52]

Given the lack of a security arrangement and the involvement quandary facing the West, it is not surprising that Ukraine is dragging its heels on full nuclear disarmament and appears intent on holding onto many of its 'inherited' Russian nuclear missiles on Ukrainian soil, particularly the 46 newer SS-24s, allowed under Start-1, which run on solid fuel and do not require as much maintenance from Russian technicians.

The Economist also cites economic reasons, wryly noting, "The one economic policy the government and parliament have followed consistently is to try to use the nuclear missiles based in Ukraine to blackmail the rest of the world for handouts of cash." [53.]

Acknowledging that Ukrainian fears of a re-expansionist Russia "cannot be dismissed," The Economist notes that "being nuclear is popular: a recent poll showed that 29 per cent of Ukrainians think the country should declare itself a nuclear state and 32 per cent think it should not give up weapons without security guarantees." [54.]

The Krasnaya zvezda reports that Ukraine is forcing many of the Russian experts overseeing missiles in Ukraine to swear an oath of allegiance to Ukraine.

Many are refusing and needed upkeep of missiles is being ignored. The publication concludes "it can be said without exaggeration that the effective dismissal of specialists who refuse to swear loyalty to Ukraine could lead to a disaster worse than Chernobyl: About 500 nuclear warheads have piled up in the storage facilities – six to eight times the norm." 55.

Recalling that Ukraine also has Europe's second-largest army, the Economist suggests "rivalries between the mainly Ukrainian west of the country and the Russia-facing east, home to much of the most hopeless smokestack industry, could easily turn ugly." 56.

At the core of Ukrainian fear and distrust of Russia is an historical experience of the forced famines, the Ukrainian Holocaust, rivalling – indeed even surpassing – Hitler's horrific Jewish Holocaust in its mass destruction and oppression.

Of Josef Stalin's 1932 forced famine of Ukrainian peasants, writer and survivor Bohdan Krawchenko recounts that Ukrainians "died agonising deaths in the millions... ultimately eliminated by troops and the police by means of mass executions." 57.

Describing Stalin's vile program as "probably the greatest man-made famine in history," writer Alex De Jonge suggests Stalin simply "used his power to create a certain kind of state, one with its roots deep in Russia's past, combining elements of the Russia of Nicholas I, Peter the Great and Ivan the Terrible." 58.

Brzezinski asserts that "it is no exaggeration to state that the ultimate power of life and death in the Soviet state for about a quarter of a century was in the hands of a small band of ruthless conspirators, for whom the infliction of death on countless thousands of alleged 'enemies of the people' was a minor bureaucratic act... one will never know the full measure of Stalin's killings." 59.

The Stalin era marked only the most horrific episode in a long history of Ukrainian subjugation by Russia and the Russia-centred Soviet Union. As the former breadbasket of the USSR, Ukraine has an enviable agricultural and resource-based importance that has long made it a tempting take-over target for Russia. These fears also represent a security threat to Russia, as innocuous Russian actions are apt to be interpreted in the harshest light possible. A weak Ukrainian economy adds to the volatility.

In fact, Ukraine embodies The Economist's recipe for disaster: "Take a big country, give it an atrocious government, watch the economy go to pot, throw in nuclear weapons and a restless Russian neighbour – and start to worry." 60.

A Russia-Ukraine security dilemma is clearly the biggest non-domestic security threat facing Russia.

Internally, the risk of fascists assuming more power in Russia and making good on Zhirinovsky's threats cannot be overstated.

Nuclear missiles in the two countries and the ownership issue over those in Ukraine have strained relations and open the risk of either side resorting to the nuclear option should tensions escalate.

Russia's potential international security problems are not, unfortunately, confined to tenuous Russia-Ukraine relations. In the early 1990s, Nezavisimaya gazeta reported that Russia is expressing concern and is calling for an end of hostilities in the ongoing conflict between Azerbaijan and Armenia, accompanied by veiled threats of Russian intervention. 61.

At the same time, Izvestia reported (on a threat that still exists in the year 2003): that Russian peacekeeping forces are having difficulty maintaining order in Georgia where renewed civil war is a constant threat. 62.

And, nearly 10 years prior to the Sept. 11, 2001 attack on New York and subsequent war in Afghanistan, there existed compelling evidence that Russia may yet get drawn into yet another conflict: The Current Digest of the Post-Soviet Press and Novaya yezhednevnaya gazeta obtained information from a number of sources, including the former KGB, confirming that Uzbekistan is interfering in war-torn Afghanistan, having "enthusiastically picked up the relay baton dropped by the Soviet Union." The Current Digest also observed that g un-running Uzbek military officials "have begun to regard the northern zone of Afghanistan, which is populated by ethnic Uzbeks, as their own private domain." 63.

If Ukraine, traditionally the breadbasket for much of Eastern Europe and Russia, looks appealing to die-hard Russian Imperialists, oil-rich Kazakhstan must be particularly tempting. The Economist notes that only 43% of Kazakhstan's people are Kazakhs while a huge minority of 36% are ethnic Russians – including Russian right-wing extremist Zhirinovsky who was raised in the capital of Alma Ata in the south. The north of Kazakhstan borders Russian Siberia and is home to pro-Russian separatists.

Describing Kazakhstan as a "still shaky place" that has never known democracy, The Economist observes that the country is coping with ethnic volatility, a weak economy and strained relations with Russia. 64.

Even the welcome, stabilizing influence of Germany needs shoring up. As Asmus, Kugler and Larrabee note, "while Germany remains preoccupied with the staggering challenge of the political and economic reconstruction of its eastern half, the need to stabilize its eastern flank is Bonn's number one security concern... to protect Germany's democracy and stability." 65.

It is beyond the scope of this chapter to entertain every conceivable source of security anxiety potentially facing Russia as it is flanked by near and distant neighbours with economic instability and political volatility (Romania, for example, presents potential refugee concerns as it heads into a third year of 200%-plus inflation, economic disarray and bad government). 66.

However, China bears watching. That nation is involved in a large-scale armament build-up, with many of its latest weapons purchased at fire sale prices from Russia. It is an open question whether these many purchases – including naval armaments – constitute the overcoming of a military deficit purely in regard to China's economic size, or are instead something more sinister.

The Economist notes China's underground nuclear test in early October 1993 dashed any hopes of turning what had been a yearlong void in nuclear testing into a permanent ban and has set back global efforts to bring a halt to the spread of nuclear weapons, while further demonstrating "just how tricky negotiations will be." 67.

Even the more distant state of North Korea's secretive efforts to build the bomb may prompt nuclear programs throughout Asia and raise the threat of drawing Russian involvement.

Closer to home, Russian peace-keeping efforts at reducing Serbian aggression may yet prompt greater involvement which is bound to make the West ill at ease and could prove costly for Russia.

Serbia is a nightmare on several fronts. As the Economist notes, "Serbia has 363 quadrillion per cent inflation in addition the onslaught of a debilitating war." 68.

How Russia will be able to salvage its tenuous grip on democracy, strengthen its debilitated economy and find a suitable role on the world stage remain some of the thorniest security issues facing Russia and the West.

As Asmus, Kugler and Larrabee note:

> "Many Europeans believe that Russia is not a European country, is unlikely to become one, and should not be allowed into core European institutions. Indeed, at the moment, not a single Atlantic alliance member is in favour of allowing Russia into either the EC or NATO, although most avoid saying so openly." 69.

Asmus, Kugler and Larrabee note that "NATO needs to remain sensitive to Russia's security interests and the delicate balance of power in Moscow," and they advocate a charter relationship between NATO, the EC and Russia which would be "designed to reassure Russia that it will be included in efforts to build a new European security order." 70.

However, another political observer, Owen Harries, says it's doubtful an attempt to expand NATO eastward and offer membership to former Iron Curtain states will be accepted by Russia as "NATO is simply to take over responsibility for the stability of a region that has been in Russia's sphere of influence for centuries", and this could "provide a catalyst that would enable extreme chauvinistic elements in Russia to exploit frustrations... in ways that would have unpleasant consequences." 71.

Russia may be interested in making up lost ground. Political scientist Richard Betts raises a poignant yet chilling set of questions when he addresses the compelling dilemma of an economically weak but militarily strong Russia facing an uncertain future:

> "The concessions that happily ended the Cold War were a precipitous loss of security for Russia in the hoary terms of balance of power. The Reds may never come back, but what if the realists do? What if economic disaster, apparent failure of western liberal models, nasty manoeuvres by newly free republics, oppression of Russian minorities in those areas, and upsurge of populist and nationalist bitterness bring the principle of 'Looking out for Number One' back into favour? Will noticing that the old subservient buffer of Eastern Europe is not only gone, but aligned with the West, spur no Russian interest in rearmament?" 72.

The ominous risks Betts addresses are unquestionably real. Russia has suffered from an enormous loss of national pride after the collapse of the Soviet Union, a variation of the Russian empire, and this threw Russia sadly and somewhat unwillingly into the arms of the West.

Yet, the ongoing transition to a capitalistic, liberal-democratic society has been fraught with difficulties. Former president Yeltsin has faced an armed coup of non-democrats.

Then, fascists threatened to capture significant political power, raising dire threats of military adventurism and international armed conflict. Although a fascist regime has not yet materialized, it's clear that Russia's fragile democracy has become a convenient scapegoat for a subsidized economy, which continues to produce shoddy goods the West doesn't want.

Added to Russia's considerable internal problems, are its thorny international security concerns, particularly the uneasy neighbouring nuclear power, Ukraine.

We've also examined Russia's shaky geopolitical position as an unpredictable, volatile and extremely powerful nation surrounded by lesser states, which contribute their own nationality problems to an explosive security mix.

With its weak economy, unstable political culture, volatile society, history of oppression and growing popularity of warmongering fascists, Russia has indeed earned its unenviable position of grave concern on the international security continuum.

END NOTES:

1. Thomas Risse-Kappen, 'From Mutual Containment to Common Security: Europe during and after the Cold War', from: 'World Security: Trends & Challenges at Century's End, edited by Michael T. Klare and Daniel C. Thomas, New York: St. Martin's Press, 1991, p. 123.
2. William G. Hyland, The Cold War, Toronto: Random House, 1990, p. 200
3. IBID, p. 201.
4. Walter LaQueur, Europe In Our Time: A History: 1945-1992, Toronto: Penguin Books Canada, 1992, p. 520.
5. Martin Crouch, Revolution & Evolution: Gorbachev and Soviet Politics, Toronto: Prentice Hall, 1989, p. 177.
6. Bohdan Nahaylo and Victor Swoboda, Soviet Disunion: A History of the Nationalities Problem in the USSR, New York: The Free Press, 1989, p. 354.
7. The Economist, Dec. 11-17, 93, p. 23.
8. William G. Hyland, The Cold War, Toronto: Random House, 1990, p. 196.
9. Walter LaFeber, America, Russia, and the Cold War, New York: Alfred A. Knopf Publishers, 1985, p. 3.
10. Zbigniew Brzezinski, The Grand Failure: The Birth and Death of Communism in the Twentieth Century, New York: Macmillan Publishing Company, 1990, p. 1.
11. The Economist, Dec. 11-17, 93, p. 23.
12. IBID

13. The Economist, Dec. 11-17, 93, p. 24.
14. IBID, p. 25.
15. The Economist, Nov. 20-26, 1993, 57-58.
16. The Economist, October 9-15, 1993, p. 55.
17. Zbigniew Brzezinski, The Grand Failure, New York: Macmillan Pub., 1990, p. 271.
18. The Economist, Dec. 18-24, 1993, p. 13.
19. The Economist, Dec. 11-17, 1993, p. 23.
20. The Economist, October 9-15, 1993, p. 15.
21. IBID, pp. 15-16.
22. Malcolm Gray, 'After Bloody Monday: Boris Yeltsin has Routed his Foes, But Can he get Russia on the Road to Recovery?' in Maclean's, October 18, 1993, p. 38-39.
23. Izvestia, 'The Russian Mafia assembles dossiers on important officials and politicians', as translated in The Current Digest of the Post-Soviet Press, Volume XLVI no. 4, February 23, 1994, p. 14.
24. IBID.
25. The Economist, Dec. 18-24, 1993, 13-14.
26. IBID. p. 14.
27. IBID. p. 46.
28. IBID. p. 45.
29. IBID. p. 46.
30. IBID.
31. IBID.
32. Michael McFaul, 'Nut 'N' Honey: Why Zhirinovsky can win,' The New Republic, February 14, 1994, p. 23.
33. IBID.
34. IBID.
35. IBID.
36. IBID, p. 25.

37. Paul Quinn-Judge, 'Pantie-hero', The New Republic, February 14, 1994, p. 24.
38. IBID.
39. The Economist, Dec. 18-24, 1993, p. 14.
40. The Economist, March 12-18, '94, p. 36
41. William G. Hyland, The Cold War, Toronto: 1990, 1991, p. 202.
42. Ronald D. Asmus, Richard L. Kugler and F. Stephen Larrabee, 'Building a New NATO', in: Foreign Affairs, Sept./Oct. 1993, p. 29.
43. Zbigniew Brzezinski, The Grand Failure, New York: Macmillan Pub., 1990, p. 264.
44. Ronald D. Asmus, Richard L. Kugler and F. Stephen Larrabee, 'Building a New NATO', in: Foreign Affairs, Sept/Oct. 1993, p. 30.
45. IBID. p. 29.
46. IBID.
47. IBID, p. 30.
48. IBID, p. 38.
49. Richard K. Betts, 'Systems for Peace or Causes of War?: Collective Security, Arms Control and the New Europe', International Security, Summer 1992, Vol. 17 No. 1, 22.
50. IBID.
51. The Economist, Nov. 27-Dec. 3, 1993 p. 55.
52. R. Asmus, R. Kugler and F. S. Larrabee, 'Building a New NATO', in: Foreign Affairs, September/October 1993, p. 38.
53. The Economist, Nov. 17-23, 1993. p. 17.
54. The Economist, Nov. 27-Dec. 3, 1993 p. 55.
55. Krasnaya zvezda, '43rd Missile Army is being destroyed, alarm over nuclear weapons in Ukraine is growing', in: The Current Digest, Vol. XLVI, No. 4, Feb. 23, 1994, p. 27.

56. The Economist, Nov. 17-23, 1993. p. 17.
57. Bohdan Krawchenko, Social Change and National Consciousness in Twentieth-Century Ukraine, London: Macmillan Press Ltd., 1985, p. 128.
58. Alex De Jonge, STALIN and the shaping of the Soviet Union, Glasgow: William Collins and Sons, 1986, p. 512.
59. Zbigniew Brzezinski, The Grand Failure, New York: Macmillan Pub., 1990, p. 23.
60. The Economist, Nov. 17-23, 1993. p. 17.
61. Nezavisimaya gazeta, 'Russia concerned about Baku's military successes', translated in The Current Digest, Vol. XLVI, No. 4, Feb. 23, 1994, p. 25.
62. Izvestia, 'Peace supported by bayonets cannot last forever', translated: The Current Digest, Vol. XLVI, No. 4, Feb. 23, 1994 25.
63. Novaya yezhednevnaya gazeta, 'Uzbek trail in Afghanistan', translated, and added to in: Current Digest of the Post-Soviet Union, Vol. XLVI, No. 4, Feb. 23, 1994, p. 16.
64. The Economist, March 12-18, 1994, p. 42.
65. R. D. Asmus, R. Kugler and F. S. Larrabee, 'Building a New NATO', in: Foreign Affairs, September/October 1993, p. 34.
66. The Economist, December. 18-24, 1993, pages 49-50.
67. The Economist, October 9-15, 1993, p. 18.
68. The Economist, October 9-15, 1993, p. 60.
69. R. Asmus, R. Kugler and F. S. Larrabee, 'Building a New NATO', in: Foreign Affairs, September/October 1993, p. 37.
70. IBID.

71. Owen Harries, 'The Collapse of 'The West', in: Foreign Affairs, Volume 72, No. 4, September/October, 1993, p. 42.

72. Richard K. Betts, 'Systems for Peace or Causes of War?: Collective Security, Arms Control and the New Europe', in: International Security, Summer 1992, Vol. 17 No. 1, p. 36.

BIBLIOGRAPHY

1. Asmus, Ronald D., Kugler, Richard L., and Larrabee, F. Stephen, 'Building a New NATO', in Foreign Affairs, September/October 93, p38.
2. Betts, Richard K., 'Systems for Peace or Causes of War?: Collective Security, Arms Control and the New Europe', in International Security, Vol. 17 No. 1, Summer 1992.
3. Brzezinski, Zbigniew, The Grand Failure: The Birth and Death of Communism in the Twentieth Century, New York: Macmillan Publishing Company, 1990.
4. Crouch, Martin, <+#>Revolution & Evolution: Gorbachev and Soviet Politics, Toronto: Prentice Hall, 1989.
5. Economist, (The), March 12-18, 1994
6. Economist, (The), December 18-24, 1993.
7. Economist, (The), December 11-17, 1993.
8. Economist, (The), November 27-December 3, 1993.
9. Economist, (The), November 20-26, 1993.
10. Economist, (The), November 17-23, 1993.

11. Economist, (The), October 9-15, 1993.
12. De Jonge, Alex, STALIN and the shaping of the Soviet Union, Glasgow: William Collins & Sons Publishers 1986
13. Gray, Malcolm, 'After Bloody Monday: Boris Yeltsin has Routed his Foes, But Can he get Russia on the Road to Recovery?' in: Maclean's, Oct. 18, 1993.
14. Harries, Owen, 'The Collapse of 'The West', in Foreign Affairs, Volume 72, No. 4, September/October, 1993.
15. Hyland, William G., The Cold War, Toronto: Random House, 1990-91.
16. Izvestia, 'Peace supported by bayonets cannot last forever', translated in The Current Digest, Vol. XLVI, No. 4, Feb. 23, 1994.
17. Izvestia, 'The Russian Mafia assembles dossiers on important officials and politicians', as translated in The Current Digest of the Post-Soviet Press, Volume XLVI no. 4, February 23,1994.
18. Krasnaya zvezda, '43rd Missile Army is being destroyed, alarm over nuclear weapons in Ukraine is growing', The Current Digest, Vol. XLVI, No. 4, Feb. 23, 1994.
19. Krawchenko, Bohdan, 'Social Change and National Consciousness' in: Twentieth-Century Ukraine, London: Macmillan Press Ltd., 1985.
20. LaFeber, Walter, America, Russia, and the Cold War, New York: Alfred A. Knopf Publishers, 1985.
21. LaQuer, Walter, Europe In Our Time: A History: 1945-1992, Toronto: Penguin Books Canada, 1992.

22. McFaul, Michael, 'Nut 'N' Honey: Why Zhirinovsky can win,' The New Republic, February 14, 1994.
23. Nahaylo, Bohdan, and Swoboda, Victor, Soviet Disunion: A History of the Nationalities Problem in the USSR, New York: The Free Press, 1989.
24. Nezavisimaya gazeta, 'Russia concerned about Baku's military successes', translated in The Current Digest, Vol. XLVI, No. 4, Feb. 23, 1994.
25. Novaya yezhednevnaya gazeta, 'Uzbek trail in Afghanistan', translated, verified and added to in The Current Digest of the Post-Soviet Union, Vol. XLVI, No. 4, Feb. 23, 1994.
26. Quinn-Judge, Paul, 'Pantie-hero', The New Republic, February 14, 1994,
Foreign Affairs, Sept./October 1993.
27. Risse-Kappen, Thomas, 'From Mutual Containment to Common Security: Europe during and after the Cold War', in World Security: Trends & Challenges at Century's End, edited by Michael T. Klare, and Daniel C. Thomas, New York: St. Martin's Press, 1991.

Chapter Four

After the Cold War:

Greece ill at ease as NATO focus changes

With the November 2002 election of Recep Tayyip Erdogan as Turkey's prime minister, Greece has lost even more status in the eyes of America and NATO.

Although pro-Islamic, Erdogan is billing himself as a moderate who would support a U.N. sanctioned war on Iraq and allow the U.S. to use Turkish airfields and airspace. Turkey's central geographic location makes it a valuable staging ground for such a war and the Americans are certain to reward Turkey in some fashion for its co-operation and support.

But as Turkey rises in stature, its historic rival, Greece, continues to fade, a process that began with the end of the Cold War.

With the fall of the Berlin Wall, November 9, 1989, came the end of the Cold War and the beginning of an uncertain post Cold War peace. The uncertainty stems from the loss of a war, which was unlike any other. With its total lack of violent conflict between the two chief superpower protagonists of the United States and Soviet Union, the 'war' was largely confined to several limited regional conflicts within a broader, somewhat tense, world peace.

With its attendant bipolarity, nuclear weapons and global balance of power, the Cold War had brought predictability and sense of certainty to the world stage: Nations were divided into clear alliances; NATO and Warsaw; us and them. The balance of threat between the superpower hegemonies worked to stop the suicidal devastation of nuclear war.

For almost half a century the world has been able to avoid another violent world war, but did the end of the Cold War mark the start of an unstable, multi-polar anarchy in which old regional conflicts – Greece and Turkey for example – suddenly re-emerge?

My analysis is that Greece is particularly vulnerable to a shift to multi-polarity and that the end of the Cold War has already cost this nation state much of the enhanced status and security it once enjoyed as a strategic member of NATO.

In the absence of a Soviet threat, Greece's geopolitical importance to NATO has been diminished and Greece can no longer assume with absolute certainty that outside aggression would necessarily be met with superpower intervention.

And, the more vulnerable Greece that has emerged following the Cold War is today highly sensitive to regional tensions and faces a serious threat of eventual involvement in a major conflict with Turkey, a neighbouring regional power and former subjugator which has retained significant strategic value to NATO – particularly post 9-11.

Citing numerous experts, this chapter will illustrate the complexities of Greek's security problems as they relate to a weak domestic economy, shrinking strategic importance to NATO, uneasy entry into the European Community, volatile neighbours and unresolved territorial disputes.

To gain a fuller appreciation of the intricacies and resiliency of security problems associated with the unenviable Greek position in the post Cold War age; it's worth reflecting on the nation's conflict-ridden modern history.

In 1453, the Byzantine Empire - with Greece at its heart - ended. The Turks took over Greece, making it part of the Ottoman Empire.

The take-over by the Turks began a period of almost 400 years of oppressive Turkish rule, the aftermath of which continues to taint Greek-Turkish relations today with territorial disputes and mutual distrust. 1.

During the Ottoman Empire, war altered borders and displaced peoples. Greeks were left to share northern lands with Albanians while sharing Macedonia with Slavs. The foundations were laid for modern day disputes over rights to ancient territories. 2.

In 1822, Greece rose against the Turks and declared independence but the Turks refused to recognize an independent Greece and a 7-year war ensued. The strength of the Turkish power was evident even then.

Greece eventually won against the larger and stronger Turkey - but only with the help of Great Britain, France and Russia. 3.

After winning independence in 1829, Greece became a kingdom under Otto of Bavaria, but with a reduced landmass, leaving two-thirds of Greeks living outside Greece. This situation proved intolerable for the Greeks and in the ensuing decades, Greece gave top priority to reuniting Greeks and former territories. 4.

In 1864, Britain turned over to Greece the Greek-populated Ionian Islands and in 1897, Greece tried to seize from Turkey the island of Crete - where numerous Greeks live - but Turkey won the war. Greece was nearly wiped out until aid was obtained from Russia, Great Britain, Austria-Hungary and Germany. 5.

Then the Greco-Turkish War broke out in 1897 with Greece embroiled in a struggle for influence in Macedonia to help Greeks living there fend off Serbian and Bulgarian guerrilla bands. On a second front, Greece struggled to take over the predominantly Greek island of Crete but the Turks again later won it back.6.

In 1912, the Balkan Wars erupted and Greece, allies Serbia, Bulgaria and Montenegro, managed to defeat the ever-powerful Turkey in two wars, in 1912 and 1913. Greece won Crete, other islands and part of Macedonia. 7.

After three years of neutrality, Greece entered the First World War fighting German allies Turkey and Bulgaria. At war's end in 1919, Greece was awarded the Turkish city of Smyrna, which had been a Greek colony for hundreds of years before the birth of Christ and still had a large, Greek-speaking population. 8.

Three years later, the Turks retook Smyrna and the Greeks lost yet another war to Turkey. 9.

In recognition of Turkish supremacy in the region, the 1923 Treaty of Lausanne made Greece give up territorial claims on Turkey. Left unsolved were Greek claims to southern Albania. 10.

In 1924 Greece declared itself a republic but after internal upheaval, King George II ended a parliamentary deadlock by appointing Metaxas premier for life and Greece, the cradle of democracy, became a dictatorship. 11.

By 1932, massive debt and inflation had led Greece to declare bankruptcy. Greece also had a shaky currency and internal unrest.

After another attempt at neutrality, Greece entered World War II in 1939 after being attacked by the Italians. Greece forced the Italians to retreat and captured half of Albania until Germans and Bulgarians captured Greece and occupied it for the final three years of the war until the Allies freed it. 12.

In 1946, Greece was immersed in a civil war in which Communists in Greece, backed by Yugoslavia, Bulgaria and Albania attempted to install a Communist dictatorship. It had been organized by Russia, thus fuelling the Soviet expansionism fears of the Cold War. 13.

In 1949, Yugoslavia broke with Russia and ended its help of Greek Communists. Greece finally put down the rebels later that year, led by Greek Army leader Alexander Papagos (elected premier in 1952). 14.

The U.S., alarmed by the attempted Communist take-over, replaced the financially strapped British in aiding Greece and sent an initial $400 million US in aid.

Having so far briefly reviewed a number of key developments during some 600 years of Greek history leading to the Cold War, several important lessons can be learned from this exercise.

First, it's clear Greece bears the legacy of centuries of conflict with its neighbours, resulting in deeply rooted, bitter divisions over territory and well-founded concerns over potential security threats from rival states.

Second, centuries of armed conflicts and shifting borders have left neighbouring states as well as Greece in a strong position to make claims on land, supported by history. This has made disputes all the more difficult to resolve.

Third, after being subjugated by the Turks for almost 400 years, the Greeks have marked their independence with a series of Greco-Turkish clashes and wars in which Greece has consistently been forced to rely on the help of greater powers to survive against Turkey. Based on this evidence, it's clear the antagonistic relationship with Turkey poses the greatest single security threat to Greece.

Fourth, others can easily view Greece itself as a security threat. Greek reunification efforts, through Turkish and Albanian eyes, equate to naked expansionism.

Past invasions by Greece of Turkey, Albania and Macedonia are reminders of this threat while Greece's political instability – including civil war and dictatorships – has done nothing to ease such concerns.

The shared distrust makes all of these states vulnerable to a security dilemma in which the others may view even purely defensive and innocent measures taken by one as a potential threat. Such a situation then opens up the added risk of escalating tensions and violent response.

The four lessons just outlined are at the heart of Greek's security problem; that of a vulnerable, economically weak nation state amid historically hostile neighbours.

This regional security problem was masked by the overlay of the Cold War, which made uneasy allies of Greece and Turkey within the larger struggle between superpowers. Left unresolved were land disputes.

Regarding historical claims to Cyprus, Donald Horowitz notes, "the Turks have been on Cyprus since about 1571, but the Greeks have been there longer." 15.

In replacing the British as the influential power and aid-giver to Greece, U.S. President Harry Truman made a colourful 1947 speech to convince Congress to free up hundreds of millions of dollars in aid for Greece and Turkey. In so doing, he invented what is now known as the Truman Doctrine: The stated need to protect the freedoms of Americans by protecting the freedoms of others in a global struggle between liberty and dictatorship. 16.

From the onset of its friendly overtures to Greece, the U.S. eagerly added Turkey to its regional program in an effort to gain the strategic benefits inherent in a close association with a regional power, which bordered both the Soviet Union and the Middle East.

In 1952, Greece joined NATO, but the full sense of security which might otherwise have accompanied such a powerful alliance was diminished by one important factor: Turkey had also joined NATO and its dual geopolitical importance as a regional power bordering the USSR *and* Middle East meant that it was, from the beginning, of more value to NATO.

Turkey joined NATO primarily because it held a healthy distrust of the Russians after fighting no fewer than 13 wars with them.

NATO saw both countries as providers of a powerful wedge, blocking the projection of Soviet power into the Aegean. Since the Soviet Union used these waters for half of its imports and exports, the new allies could also be called on to assist in a blockade should such a move be considered necessary by NATO. 17.

Control of the Mediterranean also means access to the Persian Gulf, which contains half of the world's known oil reserves. Military oil consumption would triple in wartime, making access to oil vital. Thus, several compelling reasons lay behind Nato's willingness to help build up both countries militarily, beyond the obvious advantage of a first line of defence against USSR expansionism in that region.

Greece and Turkey rapidly became beneficiaries of heavy investment by the U.S. in their military and security apparatus. 18.

But while the Cold War masked and possibly dampened tensions between Greece and Turkey, it did not erase them. As Barry Buzan notes: "Enmity can be particularly durable when it acquires a historical character between peoples, as it has between Greeks and Turks..." 19.

In fact, Greece and Turkey resisted the calming tendency of the larger superpower rivalry of the Cold War to "overlay" and suppress regional conflicts. As Buzan ominously observes: "The direct presence of the superpowers effectively suppressed virtually all of the previously existing local patterns of hostility for more than four decades. Only the hostility between Greece and Turkey managed to prevail openly against it." 20.

A measure of that resilient Greco-Turkish animosity became apparent in 1954 with the first of several Cold War era clashes between Greece and Turkey over Cyprus.

Cyprus, a former British colony and island off the coast of Turkey is about four-fifths Greek and one-fifth Turkish, a population mix which led to Cypriot demands in 1954 for union with Greece. In a serious miscalculation of Turkish resolve, Greece supported the idea of union – and Turkey sent in occupying troops for the first time since 1878. 21.

The British tried to resolve the situation by allowing Cyprus to become independent in 1960 but this led to fighting in 1963 between Greek and Turkish Cypriots over respective rights. Greece and Turkey lined up on opposite sides in the dispute, with Turkey bombing Greek strongholds in Cyprus. 22.

The world was pushed very close to war until both Cypriot factions agreed to a United Nations cease-fire. 23.

In 1967, a military coup put Greece under a 7-year military dictatorship. As Walter Laqueur observed: "Civil liberties ceased to exist in the very country in which the term 'democracy' had been coined." 24.

Greece backed a 1974 coup on Cyprus to put control of the island with Greek Cypriots. Turkey retaliated by invading Cyprus and conquering 40 per cent of the island. During this crisis, democracy was restored in Greece which narrowly avoided war with Turkey. 25.

Indeed, even the Cold War alliance of Greece and Turkey was not enough to stop confrontations with potentially serious repercussions from occurring over Cyprus.

Yet, the Cold War importance of the two nations drew intervention from the British, the Americans and the U.N. - if only to keep the alliance in place. As James Brown suggests: "...The overriding United States concern was not the rights or wrongs of either side or the fate of the two communities on the island, but rather the way to limit the potential damage to NATO and its strategic position in the Mediterranean. Thus the U.S. sought to defuse the situation and, above all, to prevent a war between Turkey and Greece that would be disastrous for all concerned. It did nothing to further a permanent solution to the Cyprus problem." 26.

And Turkey has not hesitated to push its interests forward at the expense of Greece.

Militarily powerful and economically weak, Turkey is set apart from neighbouring Middle-Eastern states by its European outlook, its secular, democratic state (despite its new Islamic government) and its lack of oil. As Morris Singer points out, Turkey produces only 15 per cent of its own crude oil- and this has "contributed greatly to its economic woes." 27.

In 1973, Turkey sought to address its oil dependency problems by unilaterally granting itself oil exploration licenses on the Aegean continental shelf claimed by Greece. 28.

Disputes also arose over airspace rights, militarization of islands and Turkish demands for shared sovereignty of waters Greece deems its own. The Turks made it clear they prefer political or military solutions to disputes instead of abiding by existing international rights-of- the-sea rules, which favour Greece. 29.

The end of the Cold War made Greece more vulnerable to Turkish acts of aggression as Greece lost its strategic importance as a wedge against Soviet penetration of the Aegean while Turkey has retained its importance as an influential bridge to the Middle East.

Based on this remarkable shift in strategic importance, it is likely that the United States and Nato will be reluctant to risk alienating Turkey by overtly supporting Greece in Greco-Turkish disputes.

In an effort to retain Turkey as an ally, the U.S. can be expected to continue advocating negotiated settlements while avoiding giving Greece the stronger support it seeks.

As we've seen from our review of Greek-Turkish history, Greece has historically been too weak to battle a powerful Turkey without the intervention of other powers. That situation has not changed: Turkey is today a regional military power with a population six times that of Greece.

On January 1, 1981, the 10 million citizens of Greece took a collective step forward by making their nation the 10th member of the European Economic Community. 30.

Yet, the post Cold War stability that EC membership could offer was immediately under strain. The other European nations voiced reservations about letting Greece into the EC, given Greece's weak economy and inflation rate, then hovering around 14 per cent. 31.

Greece has suffered recurring economic problems flowing from high unemployment and from massive numbers of individuals and businesses evading its steep taxes. 32.

Thus, Greece's uneasy membership in the EC along with its post Cold War domestic and economic problems have left it ill-prepared to deal with an array of threats from Turkey, a militarized society with the second-largest army in NATO.

Turkey has itself shown past political instability and has been ruled by military dictatorships on several occasions. 33.

Relations are also less than ideal with Albania, a former Soviet puppet state known for meddling in the affairs of neighbouring states. As recently as the 1980s, the former Yugoslavia accused Albania of using a clandestine Marxist-

Leninist group in an attempt to establish an Albanian republic in Yugoslavia. 34.

With the end of the Cold War, the Americans have removed many of their military bases, thus reducing the amount of military protection readily available to Greece. 35.

Albanians have clashed with Serbians over the Kosovo region of the former Yugoslavia, which Serbia considers its own.

Albania has accused the Serbs of exploiting Albanians who comprise 77 per cent of Kosovo region population.

Kosovian demands for an independent republic have been met in the past with Serbian tanks and paratroops. 36.

In the early 1990s, Albania complained of Serbian persecution of ethnic Albanians in Kosovo and the U.S. threatened retaliation if Serbian interference continued. 37.

There is a risk that disputes between Albania and its neighbours could flare up again, sending waves of refugees into Greece and straining the country's frail economy.

Tensions continue between Serbs and Albanians. The Economist correctly predicted that after other wars in ex-Yugoslavia end, the dispute in Kosovo "will bubble on." 38.

Greece's relations with Albania recently hit a new low when the now-defeated conservative government of Greece began advocating autonomy for southern Albania's Greek minority.

Albania has countered by reducing the numbers of its Greek language schools. 39.

Observing "Greece's relations with Albania have rarely been worse," The Economist was, by the early 1990s, reporting, "Ugly incidents on the border are now more frequent." 40.

Meanwhile, conflict between expansionist Serbians and Croatians remains immensely destructive.

The bloody conflict with its 'ethnic cleansing' has resulted in the displacement of thousands of citizens of former Yugoslavia. 41

Again, the direct threat to Greece from this is one of mass migrations of people to Greece.

As for Macedonia itself, the mere existence of this partly Greek, partly Slavic state is fuelling fears in Greece over recognition of the Macedonia name. 42.

Greece has repeatedly stressed that if it recognizes the state to the north as Macedonia, this will open the risk of that state claiming the Macedonia region of northern Greece. 43.

As The Economist notes: "Greece refuses to recognize its northern neighbour on the argument that in some future Balkan upheaval, its own province of Macedonia might be claimed by hostile Slavs as part of a greater Macedonia." 44.

The end of the Cold War has left Greece particularly vulnerable to northern border disputes with Albania and Macedonia while its fragile economy is ill prepared to accommodate potential mass migrations of Balkan refugees.

The Cold War had made allies of Greece and Turkey, uniting them against a common Soviet threat. Greece and Turkey had comprised a somewhat managed security complex, each providing both a source of security and threat to the other.

Yet as we've seen, even the formidable Soviet threat did not entirely prevent potentially disastrous clashes from occurring between the two regional rivals. In the absence of the Soviet threat, the potential for less-restrained confrontations between Greece and Turkey has escalated.

As long as Nato regarded Greece and Turkey as strategically important, both countries could expect intervention by the U.S. and the U.N. to prevent their animosity from reaching tragic proportions. This intervention can no longer be viewed as a certainty.

Today, Turkey presents the primary threat to Greece and the larger nation has given every indication it will continue to unilaterally challenge Greek land, sea and air sovereignty.

There is now the added risk that such actions - short of armed aggression - may be condoned by NATO to retain Turkey as an ally. Although the strategic importance of Greece has greatly diminished, Turkey, significantly, has retained its value as an influential regional power and bridge to the Muslim world with strong trade ties to Arab nations.

For all of the reasons cited in this chapter, the end of the Cold War has worsened the Greek security situation and left Greece with an uncertain and fearful future.

Semi-circled by untrustworthy, volatile and potentially hostile states, Greece has been left in vulnerable position, exacerbated by the end of the Cold War and the loss of strategic importance to Nato that has followed.

End Notes:

1. Encyclopedia Americana; International Edition, 1980, ed., s.v. Greece. p. 354.
2. The World Book Encyclopedia, 1976, ed., s.v. Greece- Modern History. p. 412.
3. IBID, p. 415.
4. Encyclopedia Americana; International Edition, 1980, ed., s.v. Greece. p. 355.
5. IBID.
6. The World Book Encyclopedia, 1976, ed., s.v. Greece-Modern History, p.418.
7. IBID.
8. IBID.
9. Desmond Stewart and the editors of Life, Turkey, New York: Time Inc., 1965, p. 74.
10. Gerasimos T. Soldatos, 'The Inter-War Greek Economy: Income Inequality and Speculation, from European History Quarterly, Vol. 23, No. 3, July 1993, pp. 360-365.
11. IBID.

12. IBID, pp. 365-367.
13. Barbara Jelavich, History of The Balkans, Twentieth Century, Cambridge: Cambridge University Press, 1983. Pp. 306-314.
14. IBID.
15. Donald Horowitz, 'Ethnic and Nationalist Conflicts', from World Security: Trends & Challenges at Century's End, edited by Michael T. Klare and Daniel C. Thomas. New York: St. Martin's Press, 1991. p. 230.
16. Joseph S. Nye, Jr., Understanding International Conflict, New York: Harper-Collins College Publishers, 1993. Pp. 106-107.
17. Walter LaFeber, America, Russia and the Cold War, New York: Alfred A. Knopf Publishers, 1985. Pp. 49-58.
18. Ethan Barnaby Kapstein, The Political Economy of National Security: A Global Perspective, Toronto: McGraw-Hill, Inc., 1992. p. 152.
19. Barry Buzan, People, States & Fear, Boulder, Colorado: Lynne Rienner Publishers, 1991. p. 190.
20. IBID, p. 215.
21. Van Coufoudakis, 'Greek-Turkish Relations, 1973-1983: The View from Athens', from International Security, Vol. 9 No. 4, spring, 1985. Pp. 185-191.
21. Desmond Stewart and the editors of Life, Turkey, New York: Time Inc., 1965, p. 122.
23. IBID.
24. Walter Laqueur, Europe In Our Time, Toronto: Penguin Books Canada, 1992. p. 396.
25. Van Coufoudakis, 'Greek-Turkish Relations, 1973-1983: The View from Athens',
From International Security, Vol. 9 No. 4, Spring, 1985. Pp. 195-197.

26. James Brown, 'Turkey's Policy in Flux', from Current History, January 1982. p. 28.
27. Morris Singer, 'Turkey in Crisis', from Current History, January 1991. p. 27.
28. Van Coufoudakis, 'Greek-Turkish Relations, 1973-1983: The View from Athens',
From International Security, Vol. 9 No. 4, Spring, 1985. Pp. 195-197.
29. IBID.
30. Keesing's Contemporary Archives, February 6, 1981. p. 30639.
31. The Economist, November 6, 1993. p. 68.
32. The Economist, August 15, 1992. p. 40.
33. Keesing's Contemporary Archives, January 2, 1981. p. 30640.
34. Keesing's Contemporary Archives, July 3, 1981. p. 30951
35. The Economist, November 6, 1993. p. 62.
36. Keesing's Contemporary Archives, July 3, 1981. p. 30951.
37. IBID, pp. 30949-30950.
38. The Economist, July 24, 1993. p. 55.
39. The Economist, November 6, 1993. p. 68.
40. The Economist, November 6, 1993. p. 62.
41. The Economist, October 10th, 1992. p. 64.
42. The Economist, Sept. 11th, 1993. p. 53.
43. The Economist, Nov. 6, 1993. Pp. 62-68.
44. The Economist, October 24th, 1992. p. 60

Manor House Publishing
(905) 648-2193